T&T CLARK STUDY GUIDES TO THE OLD TESTAMENT

AMOS

Series Editor
Adrian Curtis, University of Manchester, UK
Published in Association with the Society for Old Testament Study

Other titles in the series include:

1 & 2 Samuel: An Introduction and Study Guide
1 & 2 Kings: An Introduction and Study Guide
Ecclesiastes: An Introduction and Study Guide
Exodus: An Introduction and Study Guide
Ezra-Nehemiah: An Introduction and Study Guide
Hebrews: An Introduction and Study Guide
Leviticus: An Introduction and Study Guide
Jeremiah: An Introduction and Study Guide
Job: An Introduction and Study Guide
Joshua: An Introduction and Study Guide
Psalms: An Introduction and Study Guide
Song of Songs: An Introduction and Study Guide
Numbers: An Introduction and Study Guide

T&T Clark Study Guides to the New Testament:

1&2 Thessalonians: An Introduction and Study Guide
1 Peter: An Introduction and Study Guide
2 Corinthians: An Introduction and Study Guide
Colossians: An Introduction and Study Guide
Ephesians: An Introduction and Study Guide
Galatians: An Introduction and Study Guide
James: An Introduction and Study Guide
John: An Introduction and Study Guide
Luke: An Introduction and Study Guide
Mark: An Introduction and Study Guide
Matthew: An Introduction and Study Guide
Philemon: An Introduction and Study Guide
Philippians: An Introduction and Study Guide
Romans: An Introduction and Study Guide
The Acts of the Apostles: An Introduction and Study Guide
The Letters of Jude and Second Peter: An Introduction and Study Guide

AMOS

An Introduction and Study Guide
Justice and Violence

By
Walter J. Houston

Bloomsbury T&T Clark
An imprint of Bloomsbury Publishing Plc

B L O O M S B U R Y
LONDON • OXFORD • NEW YORK • NEW DELHI • SYDNEY

Bloomsbury T&T Clark

An imprint of Bloomsbury Publishing Plc

Imprint previously known as T&T Clark

50 Bedford Square	1385 Broadway
London	New York
WC1B 3DP	NY 10018
UK	USA

www.bloomsbury.com

BLOOMSBURY, T&T CLARK and the Diana logo are trademarks of Bloomsbury Publishing Plc

First published 2015. This edition published 2017

British Library Cataloguing-in-Publication Data
A catalogue record for this book is available from the British Library.

ISBN: PB: 978-1-3500-0899-1
ePDF: 978-1-3500-0901-1
ePub: 978-1-3500-0900-4

Library of Congress Cataloging-in-Publication Data
A catalog record for this book is available from the Library of Congress.

Series: T&T Clark Study Guides to the Old Testament, volume 26

Cover design: clareturner.co.uk

Typeset by Newgen Knowledge Works (P) Ltd., Chennai, India
Printed and bound in Great Britain

CONTENTS

Part I
READING AMOS

Part II
WRITING AMOS

Part III
Amos Read

PREFACE

It was my work on concepts of justice in the Hebrew Bible (Houston 2008) that led me to volunteer to write the volume on Amos at the moment that the Phoenix Old Testament Guides project was launched by the Society for Old Testament Study in succession to their older Old Testament Guides series. In that earlier work, I had chosen Amos as representative of the prophetic denunciation of social injustice for the obvious reason that social injustice is the main, and arguably the only, reason offered by the book for the destruction that it announces as the fate of the kingdom of Israel. That thought still lay before me as I worked on the present Guide in fulfilment of my offer and commission. As I document in the final chapter here, the book of Amos has in recent centuries been an inspiration to readers committed to struggle against injustice in their own societies, even though they may not share the book's conception of divine action or of the connection between moral evil and suffering. I hope and pray that this Guide may not only fulfil its primary function of helping students in the study of the book, but also assist readers inspired by Amos in that way to a deeper and more critical understanding of his prophecy.

I am grateful to the editor of the series, Adrian Curtis, for his patience in waiting for a somewhat delayed manuscript, and for his wise and helpful comments, which have made the work more user-friendly. My wife Fleur, as always, has supported me throughout with her loving interest and encouragement, and I offer her my gratitude and love.

Walter J. Houston
12 March 2015

ABBREVIATIONS

This list does not include abbreviations of the names of biblical books or of American States, nor well-known and widely used abbreviations such as 'e.g.'

ATD	Das Alte Testament Deutsch
BBB	Bonner Biblische Beiträge
BCE	before the common era (= BC)
Bib	*Biblica*
BibInt	*Biblical Interpretation*
BT	*The Bible Translator*
BTB	*Biblical Theology Bulletin*
BZAW	Beihefte zur Zeitschrift für die alttestamentliche Wissenschaft
CD	Damascus Document
CE	of the common era (= AD)
ET	English translation
FAT	Forschungen zum Alten Testament
HBT	*Horizons in Biblical Theology*
ICC	International Critical Commentary
JB	Jerusalem Bible
JBL	*Journal of Biblical Literature*
JSOT	*Journal for the Study of the Old Testament*
JSOTS	Journal for the Study of the Old Testament Supplement Series
JTS	*Journal of Theological Studies*
KAT	Kommentar zum Alten Testament
KJV	King James Version
LHBOTS	Library of Hebrew Bible/Old Testament Studies
LXX	Septuagint
NCBC	New Century Bible Commentary
NIV	New International Version
NJB	New Jerusalem Bible
NRSV	New Revised Standard Version
OPTAT	*Occasional Papers in Translation and Text Linguistics*
OTE	*Old Testament Essays*
OTL	Old Testament Library
OTS	Oudtestamentische Studien
REB	Revised English Bible
SB	Stuttgarter Bibelstudien
TZ	*Theologische Zeitschrift*
VT	*Vetus Testamentum*
VTSup	Vetus Testamentum Supplements
WMANT	Wissenschaftliche Monographien zum Alten und Neuen Testament

ZAW	*Zeitschrift für die alttestamentliche Wissenschaft*
ZDPV	*Zeitschrift des deutschen Palästina-Vereins*
ZTK	*Zeitschrift für Theologie und Kirche*

*   Against a biblical reference, this indicates that only parts of the passage are referred to.

INTRODUCTION

Why Amos?

If you are a student, Amos may be the first book of the Old Testament, or Hebrew Bible, you have been asked to read in your course, and perhaps the very first you have ever read. Others may know the Old Testament, or parts of it, well, but would like to know what it is about this book that makes it such a favourite with compilers of courses and programmes of study.

The book is short and relatively straightforward to understand, compared with some other Old Testament books, particularly prophetic ones, and there are few difficulties in its text. But I would pick out two more important reasons that make Amos distinctive. The first is that uniquely among prophetic books it makes the issue of *injustice to the poor* the main, or even perhaps the only, justification for the message of destruction that it carries. The consequence is that especially over the last 100 years or so readers of the Bible concerned with injustice in their contemporary societies have been drawn to Amos as a forerunner or model for their own religious commitment to social justice or work with the poor (see pp. 87-94).

The other reason is that Amos is 'the first of the writing prophets', as it is usually put. This is a rather misleading way of expressing it. We have no idea whether Amos himself ever wrote anything. It would be better to say that Amos is probably the earliest of the prophets who have books named after them. The book itself, as a whole, may not derive from Amos's time (see Chapter 7), but there seem to be references to it in some late prophetic writings (Isa. 65.21-22; Joel 3.16, 18; Obadiah 10). Amos thus represents the beginnings of an important stream of tradition in the literature and theology of the Hebrew Bible—to some, the most important.

These are the reasons that make Amos worth reading, and that I hope will add to the interest of your study. Before you go any further, it would be wise to read straight through Amos without stopping to ask questions—it will take you about half an hour. I suggest that after doing that you write down your immediate impressions. After that, you can go back to read it more carefully and with the help that is offered by this book.

A Preview of this Book

This book is intended to assist your study in the following ways. After this introduction, which concludes with an annotated list of books and articles that are of general value in reading Amos, there are three Parts, which correspond to the three main aspects of biblical study as it is pursued today.

Part I, 'Reading Amos', studies from various points of view *how the book of Amos makes sense, and what sense it makes*. Chapter 1 tries to answer the question 'What *kind of work* is the book of Amos?'—in technical terms, its *genre*—'and how is it written?'—its *style*.

Amos is like other books of its genre in being a composition of small pieces, a mosaic, and that will lead us to ask about the genres of the individual pieces. We shall also ask here about the way in which these pieces make an impact through the way in which they are written, covering poetry and prose, imagery, satire and word play.

Chapter 2 reverses the process of Chapter 1, by examining how the small units are linked together to make longer units that may be seen as coherent, and looking at the various suggestions that have been made as to how the whole book is *shaped* out of these units in a structured way. That naturally leads into Chapter 3, which asks what the book so structured, and with its recurring motifs, is saying as a whole, its main theme.

The last two chapters of this section deal with two essential aspects of the theme. Chapter 4 deals with the moral assumptions which justify Amos's announcements of judgment, and Chapter 5 with the beliefs about God and God's activity that the book displays.

Part II, 'Writing Amos', asks *how the book of Amos has come to be as it is*. (Of course writing comes before reading in chronological order, but *for the reader* reading the book is the experience which leads on later to trying to understand its writing.) Chapter 6 discusses the political, social and religious situation as it may be reconstructed from the historical evidence. Chapter 7 studies the various proposals for understanding how, over what period and for what purposes the book has been composed, how much of the book goes back to Amos himself, how much is the work of later editors.

Part III, 'Amos Read', has just one chapter that looks at what is called the 'reception history' of the book: *how it has been read, understood, interpreted and used or applied* in the course of history.

A couple of notes about how God is referred to in this book. The book of Amos normally refers to the God of Israel by the name which I shall spell Yhwh, since Jews since biblical times have out of reverence not pronounced it. Most English versions have 'the LORD' in small capitals; the JB and NJB have 'Yahweh', the supposed original pronunciation. Yhwh is a male deity in the Hebrew Bible, therefore it is appropriate to use masculine language to refer to him. It is only if this deity is spoken of as the God that the modern author or reader believes in that the question of gender-neutral language need arise.

General Reading

(Please see the main bibliography (pp. 97-108) for full details of works.)

a. *Commentaries in English*

Andersen and Freedman 1989. Far too long, unnecessarily wordy and repetitious and often unconvincing, it does contain useful discussions of many issues.

Coggins 2000: i-xii, 1-9, 69-170. Short commentary for the general reader; based on the assumption the book was composed in the fifth century, whatever earlier material it contains.

Cripps 1955. First published 1929 and generally outdated, it is still sometimes worth consulting.

Garrett 2008. Mainly an analysis of the Hebrew text, it also contains exegetical remarks.

Hammershaimb 1970 (Danish original 1967). Short commentary for students beginning the study of the OT with Hebrew.

Harper 1905: c-cxl, clxiv-clxxxi, 1-200. Major critical commentary, now outdated but still occasionally worth consulting. A new commentary on Amos in the same series by R.P. Gordon is in preparation.

Hayes 1988. This work by a scholar best known as a historian of ancient Israel takes a distinctive line on the political background of the prophet and the book.

Jeremias 1998 (German original 1995). An important commentary by a major scholar, but relatively short and very accessible—no Hebrew required.

Mays 1969. Relatively short critical commentary with a theological emphasis. Requires no Hebrew.

Paul 1991. Major critical commentary with focuses on language and ancient Near Eastern comparative material. Valuable for a reader with Hebrew.

Soggin 1987 (Italian original 1982). Short, but heavy going for those without Hebrew.

Wolff 1977: i-xxiv, 87-392 (German original 1969). Generally regarded as the leading critical commentary—still, probably because Paul is very conservative. Deals with the Hebrew text and uses Hebrew script throughout.

b. *Other general works in English*

Barton 2012. The only book-length work on the theology of Amos, it also deals concisely but thoroughly with the historical-critical issues. Very accessible.

Carroll R. (= Carroll Rodas) 1992. Major work setting the reading of Amos in the context of Latin American religion and politics. For advanced students.

Carroll R. 2002. Useful reference work on research and scholarship on Amos.

Coote 1981. Presents a distinctive view of the growth of the book in readable style without scholarly apparatus.

Hagedorn and Mein (eds.) 2011. A small recent collection of studies on the exegesis and reception history of Amos.

Koch 1982: 36-76. Presents a distinctive view of the theology of the book.

Linville 2008. A study of the book's language and metaphors and their resonance.

Möller 2003. A study of the rhetoric of the book and its implications for its aim and origins.

Wolff 1973. Argues a case for the source of Amos's forms of speech and ethics in tribal wisdom.

Part I

READING AMOS

Chapter 1

WHAT KIND OF BOOK IS AMOS? GENRE AND STYLE

To make sense of the book of Amos, we need to look around it, at the books that surround it in the Old Testament, from Isaiah to Malachi. These are quite different from other books of the Old Testament, but they are similar to each other in several ways—scholars say they belong to the same *genre*. Each of them is given an introduction of one or a few verses, in which it is stated or implied that the following text derives from a named person and, crucially, that its origin was with God: either the phrase 'the word of Yhwh', or a reference to (supernatural) vision appears in each introduction. These books have been deliberately collected together because they were seen as the same type of literature, and they and the persons after whom they are named are called 'the Prophets' (in the Jewish Bible 'the Latter Prophets'). The twelve short books from Hosea to Malachi, the so-called 'Minor Prophets', or the 'Twelve Prophets', were gathered together before the end of the biblical period, for all of them were written on one scroll in several examples in the Dead Sea Scrolls collection (Tov 2001: 105). Not all the persons after whom the books are named are called prophets in the book itself, and in Amos 7.14, according to many translators and commentators, Amos appears to distance himself from the title. (NRSV, e.g., translates 'I am no prophet'; but NIV has 'I was not a prophet', and implies that he became one when he was called to prophesy. See also below, pp. 67-68.) But it is an assumption in the Hebrew Bible that prophets are the only authentic mediators of God's word and will, so that a book that genuinely does this is naturally the work of a prophet (Deut. 18.9-22).

These books (Jonah excepted) are composed of a large number of short or relatively short pieces of various kinds, many of which can themselves be classified according to genre, often without any obvious links between them. In the book of Amos there are many short prophetic words (analysed in more detail below); five first-person accounts of visions (7.1-3; 4-6; 7-8; 8.1-2; 9.1-4); and one third-person narrative about Amos (7.10-17). Many of the units are presented as utterances of God. There are 146 verses in the book, 145 if the introduction, 1.1, is excluded. In at least 90 (62%) of these God is speaking. This may be indicated explicitly by such expressions as 'Thus says Yhwh' or 'says Yhwh' or 'Yhwh's word' (*n^e'um Yhwh*; this expression is very variously translated: KJV 'saith the LORD'; NRSV 'says the LORD'; REB 'This/it is the word of the LORD'; NIV 'declares the LORD'; JB 'it is Yahweh who speaks'; see Meier 1992: 298-314). But even if not, God may speak in the first person, 'I', as in, e.g., 4.12, 'because I will do this to you, prepare to meet your God, O Israel!' or 5.12, 'For I know how many are your transgressions', etc.

A more precise profile of how those who composed the book wished it to be read can be gained by analysing their introduction, 1.1. 'The words of Amos', it begins: so we are meant to read most of the book (7.10-17 perhaps excepted) as words spoken by Amos. The verse follows with Amos's profession and home town; we ignore these at this point (see Chapter 7), and go on to the clause 'which he saw concerning Israel'. This sounds odd: how can words be 'seen', if they are not written words? A very similar expression is used at Isa. 2.1: 'The word that Isaiah son of Amoz saw concerning Judah and Jerusalem.' The word translated 'saw' in both places (*ḥāzâ*) is not the normal word for 'saw'. It is associated with supernatural visions. The implication seems to be that the 'words' of Amos were received in vision, therefore from God. This explains how it is that all the 'words' of the book are words of Amos, yet 62% are plainly also words of God.

The verse concludes with a specification of the date at which Amos 'saw' these 'words'. It places Amos's activity in the last period of relative security for the Hebrew kingdoms before the onslaught of the Assyrians in the latter half of the eighth century (see Chapter 6). There is a more obvious implication in the final reference 'two years before the earthquake'. The implication in both cases is that Amos's announcements of invasion and earthquake were carried out in short order. The words of God, given through Amos, were given in order to be fulfilled, to have effect. This is clearly part of what it meant to be a 'prophet'.

So through its resemblances to other literature in the same collection and the implications of its introductory verse, the book of Amos can be defined as a *prophetic book*. This means a book giving the words of a spokesperson for God. It does not mean that the book is prophetic in the modern popular sense of foretelling the future, although that is part of what it claims.

While most scholars would accept this definition, Jason Radine has argued that Amos (and by implication all the other prophetic books of the Hebrew Bible) is not in reality a prophetic book, that is a book giving the words of a prophet, for the real collections of prophetic sayings that we have from the ancient Near East contain only one or two short, often enigmatic, sayings from each prophet, without any context. Instead, it should be assigned to a category of 'literary-predictive texts', exemplified by a number of works from ancient Mesopotamia (Radine 2010: 110-29). These are pseudo-prophecies written by scribes.

Whatever view one takes of this account of the origin of the book, it does not call for a revision of our understanding of its genre, which is defined by comparison with its neighbours in the canon, and does not depend on any particular view of its origin. The Mesopotamian texts referred to by Radine are very unlike biblical prophetic books. They do not claim to present the words of prophets; they present a continuous narrative rather than a collection of sayings; and they are specific enough about the events to enable them to be identified—contrast the vague general threats and predictions in Amos. A much closer fit in the Hebrew Bible is the second half of the book of Daniel (Daniel 7–12), which does present a view of several centuries of history as if from their beginning. Even if one believes that some or all of the sayings in Amos do not come from a historical prophet, it does not affect the genre of the book as a presentation of words claimed to be those of a prophet.

However, when I speak of 'Amos' or 'the prophet' in the rest of Part I, it should be understood that I am speaking not of the historical prophet Amos, assuming he existed, but of the character that the book sets before us as the speaker of all its 'words'. For we cannot assume that the historical Amos did speak all the words of the book (see Chapter 7), but it is convenient here to follow the lead of its introductory verse and accept an Amos who prophesied all these words to Israel. If this distinction is found difficult, it may be helpful to look at a simple account of how modern literary critics deal with the way in which a narrative text projects a narrator, distinct from the actual author: e.g. Abbott 2008: 67-80, 235.

Genres of the Small Units

I have already mentioned the *narrative* units, the five first-person vision accounts and the one third-person anecdote. We shall be discussing at a later stage what they contribute to the message of the book, and the way in which the visions are connected. Here we should just note that they follow similar patterns to units in other prophetic books.

Burke O. Long (Long 1976) classifies vision reports in the Old Testament prophets into three types, one of which is not found in Amos. The first is what he calls the 'oracle-vision'. The two visions of Jeremiah in Jer. 1.11-14 are very similar indeed to Amos's third and fourth visions (Amos 7.7-8; 8.1-2). In all four cases the prophet sees an object and Yhwh asks him 'What do you see?', and to the reply responds with a warning or announcement based on the sound of the word or the symbolism of the object. The vision is the occasion for the divine word. The other three vision reports of Amos, in 7.1-6 and 9.1-4, follow a different pattern, called by Long the 'dramatic word-vision', which describe a dramatic action, and the words spoken by Yhwh, if any, are an integral part of the drama; if the prophet speaks, that also is part of the drama. Jeremiah 4.23-26 and Ezek. 9.1-10 may be compared. But Amos's successful intercession in 7.2-3, 5-6 is I think unique as part of a vision account.

The story in 7.10-17 resembles several stories in Jeremiah where Jeremiah defends his right and duty to prophesy against those who try to silence him, e.g. Jeremiah 26.

Much the greater part of the book, however, consists of prophetic words, or 'oracles', as they are often called. The most influential form-critical analyses of these were carried out by Claus Westermann and H.W. Wolff in the middle of the last century (see Westermann 1967 and Wolff 1977: 91-98). Both scholars identified the basic genre of prophetic speech as the 'messenger speech'. Westermann argues that the expression 'thus says N' is the normal way in which messengers in the Hebrew Bible introduce the words that they have been commanded to speak, so that the common prophetic 'thus says Yhwh' implies that the words that follow are a message from Yhwh delivered by his messenger, and it is therefore described as the 'messenger formula' (Westermann 1967: 98-128).

This expression is quite common in Amos: each of the eight announcements of judgment on the nations in Amos 1–2 is introduced so, and it occurs six times more: in 3.11, 12; 5.3, 4, 16; 7.17. The majority of Yhwh's speeches, however, are indicated as such in different ways, and quite a number of Yhwh-speeches are not marked at all. (See Meier 1992: 226-29.)

But Wolff characterizes all the speeches of Yhwh in Amos, whether introduced by the so-called 'messenger formula' or not, as 'commission-bound messenger speech' (Wolff 1977: 92). More recently others have pointed out that the expression 'thus says N' does not necessarily indicate a message at all; it is simply a formula of citation: it shows that the speaker is quoting someone, but not necessarily that that person has commissioned him or her. For example, in Amos 7.11 Amaziah sends to the king, saying, 'Thus says Amos…'. Obviously this is not a message from Amos via Amaziah; Amaziah is simply quoting him (Meier 1992: 281; see Meier's whole discussion pp. 277-91). This does not affect the fact that prophetic speech in Amos and elsewhere is frequently the speech of God, but it does cast doubt on the idea that these speeches are messages in genre. In fact, there is no such genre as 'message'.

The majority of the speeches of God in Amos are proclamations of judgment, from the eight 'oracles against the nations' in chaps. 1-2 to 'I give the command' in 9.9-10. Many of them are simply announcements of the punishment to come, for example 3.11; 3.12; 3.13-15, three in a row. Others preface the announcement with an accusation which gives the reason for the judgment, such as all the eight speeches against the nations. In yet other examples, the accusation appears to be the word of the prophet speaking in his own person, who introduces with this the speech of Yhwh's judgment.

Good examples of this structure are 4.1-3, the denunciation of the 'cows of Bashan', and 8.4-7, the speech against the corn dealers. It is a frequent characteristic of Amos's accusations that he defines who he is addressing simply by listing their wrongdoings (see also 2.6b-8; 5.7; 5.10-11a; 6.1-6; 6.13).

Not all of Yhwh's words in Amos are announcements of judgment. Amos 4.4-5 is an ironical exhortation, and 4.6-12 is rather a series of rebukes climaxing in a warning, unless 'prepare to meet your God' can be seen as an announcement of judgment. Then 5.4-6 is an exhortation leading again to a warning, and 5.21-24 is a diatribe leading up to an exhortation (perhaps— see below, p. 39). It would be difficult to classify 9.7, but 9.11-12 and 13-15 are oracles of salvation, the only good news in the book.

Most of the 30 or so verses outside the narrative units in 7.1–8.2; 9.1-4 that are not words of Yhwh are classified by Wolff (1977: 93-94) as 'free witness-speech'. Some of this is 'prophetic prologue to the word of Yahweh'. We have already noted how some divine announcements of judgment are prefaced by accusations in the prophet's own words. Elsewhere, he may simply introduce them with 'Hear this word that Yhwh has spoken' (3.1), or the formula 'thus says Yhwh' (3.12), or slip in n^e'um Yhwh (e.g. 8.9, 11). There are a small number of prophetic speeches that are not connected in this way with a word of Yhwh. They take a wide variety of forms. Wolff takes note of the 'didactic questions' in 3.3-8; 5.20; 6.2, 12. These are in a way rather like parables. Although they are rhetorical questions, they demand an answer. The hearers are required to define their position in the light of the question, which is aimed to make them redefine it. Then there are the funeral dirge in 5.2, the exhortation to 'seek Yhwh' in 5.14-15, and the 'woe' sayings in 5.18-19 and 6.1-7.

Several 'rhetorical forms characteristic of Amos', including didactic questions, 'woe-cries', numerical sequences and speeches of exhortation, are seen by Wolff (1973: 6-53) as being derived from 'clan wisdom', the teaching of elders in the rural communities of Israel. Wolff connects this with the origin of Amos himself from such a community (see p. 68). But it has been questioned whether these speech types are really so specifically connected with such a setting in life, and recent writers have not continued this line of enquiry.

A question that may have occurred to you even in your first read-through of the book, and certainly now that we have looked at the great variety of genres of small units in the book is: How is it that a book that contains so many and so absolute proclamations by Yhwh himself of the disaster heading Israel's way can also contain exhortations urging them to *avoid* disaster by changing their ways, most clearly in 5.4-5 and 14-15? We shall come back to this question in Chapter 3 where we discuss the overall message of the book, but it is useful to see how it arises out of its basic material.

In addition to these prophetic words, there are three passages that appear to be fragments of a hymn or hymns of praise: 4.3; 5.8-9; and 9.5-6. They are similar to parts of a psalm of praise like Ps. 33 or 99.

Poetry and Prose

Characteristic of much prophetic literature in the Hebrew Bible is its *poetic form*. This is particularly true of the type of short oracles of which the book of Amos largely consists. Robert Alter argues that 'since poetry is our best human model of intricately rich communication, not only solemn, weighty and forceful but also densely woven with complex internal connections, meanings and implications, it makes sense that divine speech should be represented as poetry' (Alter 1985: 141). The vision accounts and third-person narrative, and the headings in 1.1, 3.1-2, etc., and introductions to divine speech, 'Thus says Yhwh' and so on, are in prose, but the majority of the book is in poetic form. In modern translations this is indicated by setting the text out in lines instead of continuously. But you will see if you compare a number of modern versions that they do not always agree on what should be set out as verse. Hebrew verse is not sharply distinguished from prose, though it has certain features that may be present in more or less strongly marked form.

Although most of the prophetic oracles are poetry, it is generally agreed that there are sentences of prose among them, but not which they are. Chapter 6, vv. 9-10 is the most obvious example, though even this is printed as verse by JB. Andersen and Freedman discuss the issue (1989: 144-49), noting that prophecy, and the prophecy of Amos in particular, tends to use a type of poetry with some prosaic features, and that this is particularly true of the formulaic series (see Chapter 2) in 1.3–2.16 and 4.6-12, and of some other passages such as 3.3-8; 5.18-20; and 9.1-4. Besides the obviously prose narrative sections, they also here identify 2.9-13 and most of chap. 9 as prose. But these are printed as verse in all the modern versions!

The question becomes important when there appear to be prose sentences sharply interrupting poetic or semi-poetic contexts (rather than being indispensable parts of them, as the charges against the nations are). None of the standard modern translations prints 2.10 as prose, but that it clearly is: it does not consist of rhythmic lines, there is no parallelism, and the expression is 'prosaic'. (See Wolff 1977: 134; Jeremias 1998: 39. They also take vv. 11-12 as prose: but v. 10 is a clearer case.) Even clearer are 3.7 and 5.25-27, unquestionably prose, though each of them is set as verse by at least three modern versions. Why these (and other) prose sentences may differ from their context will be explored below, pp. 70, 74.

Imagery

An important but variable characteristic of poetry in all languages, and typical of prophetic oracles in the Old Testament, is the use of imagery of various kinds: metaphor, simile, personification, symbol, and so forth. This is not mere decoration; imagery enriches and deepens the expression of ideas and makes connections between different realms of discourse. It makes an important contribution to the impact of the book of Amos. The simile in 5.24, for example, 'Let justice roll down like water, and righteousness like an ever-flowing stream' is justly one of the most well-known texts in Amos.

Alter identifies three 'poetic strategies' in the prophecy of condemnation: '(1) direct accusation; (2) satire; (3) the monitory evocation of impending disaster' (1985: 141). All three of these strategies are employed in Amos, and all of them use imagery or figurative language to a greater or lesser extent.

Direct Accusation

A variety of expression, much of it in figurative language, serves to accuse people in Israel of oppression and violence. If 2.6, 'they sell the righteous for silver', etc., refers to the miscarriage of justice through bribery, then it is a metaphor. But it is more frequently understood of literal selling into slavery. The following phrase 'trample the head' of the poor (into the dust?), or (understanding the Hebrew verb differently) 'pant after' them, whatever it means, is certainly metaphorical (2.7, cf. 8.4; see Coggins 2000: 104; Garrett 2008: 56-57). Garrett understands the Hebrew text as a metaphor from hunting: 'they sniff the earth (like hounds) for (the prize of) the heads of the poor'.

They 'turn aside the way of the wretched' (2.7); and in 5.12 they 'turn the needy aside in the gate' (the Hebrew verb is the same). This may be read literally: members of the arrogant governing elite shoulder the poor aside as they pass them. According to Avraham Faust destitute persons may have been accommodated in public buildings near the city gate (Faust 2012: 101-109). However, the reference to the 'gate' in 5.12 has generally been taken to refer to the court held in the square in front of the gate (cf. Ruth 4.1-12), so that to 'turn the poor aside' there would be a metaphor for depriving them of justice; and the phrase in 2.7 is usually taken to mean the same thing (Wolff 1977: 166; Jeremias 1995: 35; Garrett disagrees [2008: 59-60]).

Other images of violence and oppression are found at 3.10; 5.7; 6.12. They 'store up violence and oppression (or destruction) in their strongholds' (3.10: what they literally store up is the *proceeds* of violence and oppression). They 'turn justice to wormwood and cast righteousness to the ground' (5.7); a similar metaphor appears at 6.12: 'You have turned justice to poison, and the fruit of righteousness to wormwood.'

Satire

The arrogant behaviour of the oppressors in Israel is sketched *satirically* in a series of vivid brief scenes, using irony and exaggeration, and contrasted with their ignominious end. Those who are regarded as the 'first among the nations' (6.1) and spend their days in extravagant feasting end up as 'first among the deported' (6.7) (word play: *rē'šît haggôyim... rō'š gōlîm*). David Fishelov (1989) identifies a number of devices used in prophetic satire which involve pretending to take the point of view of the targeted persons. One is to use invented quotations to nail the malice or boasts of the target in an exaggerated or absurd way. 8.5-6 is a good example: they can't wait for the holiday to be over so that they can get back to cheating their customers. Another is at 6.13: they boast over their victories, but their own words betray how insignificant they are: many translations, e.g. NRSV, see a place name here, 'Lo-debar', but the Hebrew words can be understood as 'nothing', as e.g. KJV translates them. The second device is ironical exhortation, as at 4.4-5, encouraging them in their stupid behaviour: they so love attending the pilgrim feasts at the great temples and making a show of their piety that they sacrifice every morning, bring their annual tithes every three days (according to older commentators: see Harper 1905: 92; Cripps 1955: 170) and make public announcements of their free-will offerings (cf. Mt. 6.2!). One should be careful of taking satirical attacks literally (see Clines 1995). But satire always has a serious point and a real target, and would be pointless if the behaviour of the target bore no relation whatever to the description.

Evocations of Impending Disaster

These dominate the book. A number of *repeated* images can be included among its motifs (see Chapter 3). When you read through the book to start with, you may well have made a note of the constant appearance of images of violence, wrath or judgment. Violence characterizes the actions of both Yhwh and the culprits whom he targets. (See Mills 2010.) But the images which appear repeatedly are typical of the actions of Yhwh. Most prominent are the images of *fire*, the *lion, mourning, the sword*, and *deportation* (often translated as 'exile'). Only the second is entirely metaphorical, but none of them are invariably literal.

In each of the oracles against the nations, except the last against Israel, Yhwh announces that he will 'send fire' (at 1.14 'set fire') on their cities, walls, or houses. Is this meant literally or metaphorically? On the one hand, every invading army in those days, if it succeeded in storming a city, would set fire to it, so that a literal reading of the words is possible. On the other hand, a reading of the book as a whole will connect the fire to be sent by

Yhwh on these cities with the fire in Amos's vision of 7.4-6, which is something supernatural, cosmic in its scope, devouring 'the great deep' (see Gen. 1.2; Paul 1991: 231-32; Linville 2008: 135-37). The inextinguishable fire threatened for 'the house of Joseph' in 5.6 seems to be similar. It is not necessary to choose between literal and metaphorical readings: 'fire' whether literal or not functions as a symbol of Yhwh's wrath and judgment.

The opening oracle of the book in 1.2 says that 'Yhwh roars from Zion'; the verb refers to a lion's roar in 3.4, 8 and in many other places in the Hebrew Bible. The implied comparison of Yhwh's violence with that of a ravening lion reappears in 3.8, 12, and 5.19, and at 5.19 it is reinforced by the images of the bear and the snake. To be sure, the comparison is not explicit, but the repetition of the image leaves little doubt about what it refers to.

The image of mourning, expressing the effect of Yhwh's violence on the human and also the natural world, is another for which the opening verse of the prophecy is the springboard, with a strong personification: 'the shepherds' pastures mourn' (not 'wither', as some versions and commentators have it: see Lam. 1.4, 2.8). Mourning appears again in 8.3 and 9.5, and the image is developed into entire scenarios at 5.16-17 and 8.9-10. In 5.16-17 the noun *mispēd* 'mourning' is repeated three times over, and in 8.9, like 1.2, the mourning extends to the natural world, the sun and the earth. Amos 1.2 and 8.9 are by no means the only examples of the metaphorical or symbolic participation of the natural world in the judgment of God in Amos: see Marlow 2009: 129-57.

The motif of *the sword* appears in 4.10; 7.9, 17; 9.1, 4, 10 (omitting Amaziah's paraphrase of Amos's message in 7.11). 'The sword' of course means warfare, or death in battle, and in Amos usually implies invasion (see 3.11, 6.14). It is a *metonymy,* a word literally referring to a concrete object which is used for an institution or event with which the object is associated. But in most of these texts the sword is wielded by Yhwh himself, and thus a metonymy becomes in effect a metaphor, given that God's action has inevitably to be spoken of in human terms.

Deportation is threatened in 1.5; 5.5, 27; 6.7; 7.17. Despite the blunt predictions in 5.27 and 7.17, even this motif is not invariably to be taken literally: 'Gilgal will be deported' in 5.5 is word-play (see below) rather than a literal statement. Places or temples cannot be literally deported; but to suppose it means the inhabitants of Gilgal (Paul 1991: 163) is to miss the point, which concerns those who make pilgrimage there, not those who live there (if anybody did: see Andersen and Freedman 1989: 432).

The extended image of Yhwh's pursuit of the wrongdoers through the entire universe in Amos's final vision in 9.1-4 marks a chilling climax to the book's repeated announcements of disaster. Although the temple where Yhwh stands in 9.1 is often supposed to be that of Bethel, it has cosmic dimensions: it is at the same time both the earthly and the heavenly temple (Jeremias 1998: 156-57; see also Linville 2008: 159-60). The whole vision is of cosmic scope, and Yhwh commands the elements of the world to complete the destruction of his enemies.

Word Play

There are some clear examples of what is technically known as paronomasia, or play on words, in Amos, two of which we have already seen. At 5.5 'Gilgal shall go into exile' is in Hebrew *Gilgal gālōh yigleh*. In Amos's fourth vision, 8.2: 'summer (fruit)', which Amos sees, is *qayiṣ*; 'end' is *qēṣ*; and the words may well have been pronounced identically in the dialect of Samaria. The identically constructed third vision, 7.7-8, is likely also to involve a word play (see Paul 1991: 235 and Linville 2008: 139, following Gese 1981: 81-82).

Paul and Linville identify a great many more word plays in the text, but many of them are unconvincing. The difficulty is that they rely on the visual comparison of letters, and do not take account of the way in which literary texts were circulated in antiquity. Even the elite who could read and write encountered texts primarily in oral form, as written texts were scarce, and traditional education relied on memorization of orally recited texts (Möller 2003: 50-57; Carr 2005). Therefore paranomasia, to be effective, would have to rely on the similar *sound* of different words. *Gilgal gālōh yigleh* and *qaiṣ–qēṣ* fulfil this condition. Many of Linville's suggestions are methodologically even more problematic: they rely on various words that *may* be suggested by a word in the text, but are not actually there. The possibilities are infinite, and there are no controls.

Further Reading

Relatively little has been written on the genre 'prophetic book' as such. The collection Edelman and Ben Zvi 2009 concentrates more on the creation and historical setting of the genre than on its characteristics. But see, briefly, Ben Zvi 2005: 10-12, which defines the genre of the book of Hosea in a parallel way to my definition of the genre of Amos above; also Ben Zvi 2003.

However, on the genres of the small units, Ben Zvi is not particularly helpful: he describes the entire contents of Hosea as 'didactic prophetic readings'. Wolff's discussion in his Amos commentary (Wolff 1977: 91-100) perhaps remains the best overview, and other commentators have largely followed his analysis; while in Wolff 1973: 6-53 he deals with genres in Amos typical of wisdom at greater length. However, he only deals in either place with those units that he reckons come from Amos himself; one has to turn to 1977: 106-13 for his comments on other parts of the text (cf. p. 75).

Also, what he says about the 'messenger speech' needs to be qualified by Samuel Meier's analysis (Meier 1992).

An accessible account of Hebrew poetry for the non-Hebraist may be found in Alter 1985, and this includes a chapter specifically on 'Prophecy and Poetry' (pp. 137-62). Stephen Geller (Geller 1983) also discusses, by way of an example from Isaiah, what it might mean to call a prophet a poet in more than a purely technical sense. The use of imagery in Amos is the main subject of Linville 2008, with emphasis on its cosmic scope. Satire, specifically political satire, in the Hebrew Bible is the subject of Weisman 1998, but Amos is not dealt with extensively; however Fishelov 1989 usefully examines satire in the prophets. As I have indicated, Linville and Paul in his commentary (Paul 1991) are adept, and probably over-enthusiastic, at finding word plays in the text of Amos.

Chapter 2

THE SHAPE OF THE BOOK OF AMOS

In this and the following section we shall be making use of rhetorical analysis (see Möller 2003). The word 'rhetoric' often has a contemptuous ring to it in popular usage ('mere rhetoric'). But properly speaking it simply means the use of speech to persuade, to make a case. To analyse a text rhetorically is to work out how it makes its case. To decide on its shape or structure is a necessary part of this, since it means deciding what the rhetorical units are which need to be analysed.

The Formulaic Series

J.J.M. Roberts (1991: 9-11) says that in the typical prophetic book 'the basic unit of interpretation is the individual oracle', and that it is rare for meaning to be found over larger units than that.

The reader of Amos will not get very far before realizing that Amos is one of those allegedly rare cases. Up to this point we have been treating the book as a collection of individual units; but although each of the oracles against the nations in 1.3–2.16 is form-critically an independent unit, being introduced separately with 'Thus says Yhwh', each begins identically, 'For three transgressions of N, and for four, I will not turn it back' (whatever 'it' is), goes on to specify the wrongdoing of N and then announces the punishment, starting in very similar language except for the Israel oracle: 'I will send fire on…and it will consume its fortresses…'. The whole passage, although composed of eight separate oracles, is clearly a single composition intended to be heard as a unity. To interpret any one of them without reference to the rest would be perverse, and it is generally recognized that the whole series is intended to lead up to the final extended oracle against Israel. Often the rhetorical strategy (Möller 2003: 40-42) is understood as entrapment or surprise: a series of denunciations of the notorious war crimes of neighbouring nations traps the audience into enthusiastic agreement, until the tables are suddenly turned, their own conduct in social-class relations within the nation is put on the same level, and they are forced to confront their own 'transgressions' (Barton 1980: 3-4; Möller 2003: 191-200).

The oracles against the nations are not the only easily recognizable large-scale composition of this kind within the book of Amos. At the other end of the book we have the series of visions of Amos. The four visions in 7.1-8; 8.1-2 are invariably seen as a series, in view of their closely similar construction, despite the fact that the last two are separated by other material. Each begins 'Thus Yhwh showed me', and ends with a pronouncement by Yhwh on the future of Israel. The four obviously fall into two pairs. In the first two Amos has a vision of a disaster being prepared for Israel, and successfully intercedes with Yhwh to cancel the plan. In the third and fourth Yhwh shows him an object, and asks Amos to say what he sees; Amos's answer then leads to a pronouncement of doom. There is no agreement whether the final vision (9.1-4) is also part of the series (for: Gese 1981: 74-75, 84-85; Andersen and Freedman 1989: 834, 838; against: Hayes 1988: 216; Möller 2003: 100). It is introduced in a different way ('I saw' rather than 'Yhwh showed me'), and there is no conversation between Amos and Yhwh. However, in the first series, the oracles against the nations, we already have an example of the last member of the series diverging from the norm, and the vision can be seen as fulfilment of the judgment announced in the previous two.

Like the oracles against the nations, this series, whether or not the fifth vision is included, leads up to a climax. In the first pair, judgment is averted. The third vision is ominous, though its precise meaning is uncertain, and in the fourth Yhwh states unequivocally 'The end has come upon my people Israel.' If the fifth is included, it depicts the execution of the judgment thus announced. Again, it is easy to see how this works rhetorically as a series. By relating his private visions, and including the first pair, Amos demonstrates that he has done his best to shield Israel from Yhwh's terrible purpose. If he has become a preacher of the wrath of God, it is not because he wanted to (Jeremias 1998: 126). In the third and fourth visions, Yhwh actually traps him into pronouncing the dreadful words by presenting him with something perfectly innocent (Novick 2008). So Amos himself is innocent of malice against Israel: his character as a messenger is impartial (cf. Möller 2003: 135).

These two obvious 'formulaic series' (using regular speech formulas in successive items) have suggested a division of the book into three parts, chaps. 1-2, 3-6 and 7-9, which nearly all commentators agree on. The first part simply consists of the oracles against the nations, and the third is largely marked out by the visions, though a question arises about the place of the other material in those three chapters. But much more serious is the apparent disorder in the middle section. Are we to say that this section is a simple anthology of individual oracles as Roberts conceives it? Even that would not suffice to explain a fragment such as 5.7 or 6.13, which are not complete oracles, yet not completed by what is next to them.

But we have not finished finding formulaic series in Amos. Another obvious one is 4.6-12, where Yhwh describes five punitive interventions in the life of Israel, each one ending with the refrain 'Yet you did not return to me', and *ne'um Yhwh* marking it as an oracle of Yhwh, leading up to the climactic 'prepare to meet your God, O Israel'. The justice of the judgment is confirmed by the numerous warnings that Israel has been given.

Equally, I think, we should count the hymn-like fragments at 4.13; 5.8-9; 9.5-6, each ending 'Yhwh is his name', as a formulaic series. It is discontinuous, but we have already seen that the vision series is partially discontinuous. The placing of its members will be explained by their contexts: 4.13 and 9.5-6 each rounds off one of the other series and announce the power of the God whose judgment must now be faced, and 5.8-9 stands at the centre of another composition, as we shall see. Unlike the other series, this one crosses the boundary between two of the three main parts of the book.

H. Gese (1981) argues for a degree of symmetry between the other three series: by appealing to the widespread critical judgment that the oracles against Tyre, Edom and Judah (1.9-12; 2.4-5) are later additions (see Chapter 7, pp. 70, 73), he finds that each of the series originally had five members, arranged as two pairs and a single climax. But here it is sufficient to recognize the presence of the series, which together emphasize that the Lord of the nations intends to punish his own people, and that they should now accept the justice of that reckoning, seeing that they have failed to take advantage of the delays offered them by Yhwh's warnings and Amos's intercession.

So far we have discovered structures that cover only parts of the book. But what concerns most of those looking for structure is to find the key to how the book is organized as a whole. Is it possible to find rhetorical units linking a number of individual form-critical units in a continuous argument or thematic unity? Can order be drawn out of the apparent disorder in chs. 3–6? What accounts for the material that interrupts the series of visions in 7.9 or 7.10 to 7.17 and, if 9.1-4 counts as part of the series, 8.3 or 4 to 14? Is there a progression of thought in the book?

Chiasms and Inclusios

Since the 1970s much effort has gone into identifying recursive or 'envelope' or 'palistrophic' structures in Old Testament literature, that is, passages where material similar in form or content to the opening lines recurs at the end of the unit, or where the content of units from the beginning up to the middle recurs in reverse order from the middle to the end. It is very common in newspaper articles to finish by referring back to the case highlighted at the beginning. This is an *inclusio* (Latin for 'a shutting in'). But in order to identify one in the midst of the biblical text, we have to have some other indication that what we are looking at is a single and complete unit (not a problem with a newspaper article); otherwise we simply have a repetition.

It is more common to look for, and find, more complex recursions, which might serve to identify units in themselves. Most researchers call these '*chiasms*'. Strictly speaking, this term refers to four units in the order ABB'A', because if the second half is written under the first, and lines drawn between A and A' and B and B', the result is a cross shape like the Greek letter *chi*. But nowadays it tends to be used also where there are more than four units, sometimes many more: ABCD... N(N')... D'C'B'A'. And Amos seems to have attracted more than its fair share of such suggestions: see de Waard 1977; Smalley 1979; Lust 1981: 154; Tromp 1984 (on de Waard, Tromp and Lust see Auld 1986: 50-54); Wendland 1988; Dorsey 1992, 1999: 277-86; Noble 1995; Rottzoll 1996: 1-7. Commentators such as Andersen and Freedman and Paul mention chiastic patterns frequently, but generally small-scale ones. But see Andersen and Freedman (1989: 124), who point to an inclusio between chaps. 1 and 9.

Möller quotes Alter speaking of 'a general fondness of ancient Hebrew writers of all genres for so-called envelope structures' (Alter 1987: 621), and comments waspishly that 'it seems to me that the Hebrew writers' fondness is matched...by an even more pronounced partiality towards these devices on the part of the investigating scholar' (Möller 2003: 64-65). His scepticism seems to be justified by the fact that there is little agreement between scholars on the identification of such structures. It does not seem possible to assert confidently that they exist unless readers agree on their boundaries and the corresponding units of which they consist, and with one exception this agreement is lacking.

The Chiasm in Amos 5.1-17

The exception is the chiasm in 5.1-17 that was noticed by J. de Waard (de Waard 1977; followed by most subsequent writers, including Lust 1981; Tromp 1984; Auld 1986: 50-54; Paul 1991: 158; Jeremias 1998: 84; Möller 2003: 68-69). Why his suggestion has been so widely accepted is that it is the solution to a longstanding problem: the apparent extreme disorder of these verses, even greater than any other part of the book. Verses that seem to belong together are separated from each other, to the extent in some places of not even making grammatical sense in the Hebrew: 4-6 from 14-15, and 7 from 10-12, which is the natural continuation of v. 7; and 16 with 'Therefore' has to refer back to 12. Although v. 9 seems to be part of the hymn in v. 8, it follows the refrain 'Yhwh is his name' instead of preceding it (compare 4.13 and 9.6). Some commentators and translators even moved verses about in order to make sense (see e.g. REB). Once it is realized that the passage is a chiasm, order is restored. It is most clearly set out in diagrammatic form (after de Waard 1977: 176):

A   1-3 Mourning over Israel
B   4-6 Exhortation to seek Yhwh, and live
C   7 Injustice of some in Israel
D   8 (to 'earth') The power of Yhwh in nature
E   8 Yhwh is his name!
D'   9 The power of Yhwh over the strong
C'   10-12 (+ 13?) Judicial corruption and economic
                    oppression, and their punishment (for v. 13 see
                    Jeremias 1998: 94; Paul 1991: 175-76)
B'   14-15 Exhortation to seek good, and live
A'   16-17 Mourning in Israel

In addition, some of the individual units in this chiastic structure, or parts of them, are themselves chiastic: vv. 5-6a, 10-12, 14a + 15a. Notice how the units in the second half do not simply repeat the ideas in the first half, but develop them.

This rhetorical unit integrates in a remarkable way the proclamation of death in the A and C elements with exhortations carrying conditional promises of life in the B ones. It is now absolutely clear that this is deliberate, and not just the accidental effect of a jumble of disparate material. But which of these carries the final meaning? We can only decide that in the context of the book as a whole.

Some scholars have built on this observation to extend the chiasm in both directions. Thus Lust sees a chiasm between 4.1 and 6.7 (1981: 153-54 n. 103; or see Auld 1986: 54). The ABCC'B'A' elements here are 4.1-3 the women of Samaria, 4.4-5 against the cult, 4.6-12 (13) announcement of judgment, 5.18-20 the judgment, 5.21-7 against the cult, 6.1-7 the men of Samaria. This suggestion has been followed fairly widely (e.g. by Hadjiev, 2009: 37). Others go even further and find chiasms spanning the whole of chs. 3–6 or even the entire book (e.g. Noble 1995; Dorsey 1999: 285). These are not convincing. As Möller remarks, the larger the chiasms become, the looser the requirements for sections to be parallel need to be (Möller 2003: 68; 68-74).

Identifying Rhetorical Units

If chiasms will not work to identify the main units in 3–4; 5.18–6.14 and 8.4–9.15, what will? Möller relies largely on what he sees as opening formulas, such as 'Hear this word...' (3.1; 4.1; 5.1; cf. 8.4), or 'Woe to' (5.18; 6.1), but also even 'Yhwh showed me' (7.1) or 'I saw' (9.1). But he is also confident that he can demonstrate a continuous argument within each unit. (It is evident from the chapter divisions, first made in the Middle Ages, that medieval scholars agreed with him about 'Hear this word'.) This yields ten sections or rhetorical units: 1.1-2; 1.3–2.16; 3.1-15; 4.1-13; 5.1-17; 5.18-27; 6.1-14; 7.1–8.3; 8.4-14; 9.1-15 (Möller 2003: 89-103). Each of the opening formulas also introduces a single oracle; can they be held to 'do double duty' (Auld 1986: 57)? Several of them in any case must introduce new rhetorical units, assuming that there are such, since they follow the conclusion of a generally recognized main unit, or open one identified in other ways: this is true of 1.3; 3.1; 5.1; 5.18; 7.1; 8.4. It would seem that the editors of the book did sometimes make these phrases 'do double duty'.

Disagreement will tend to centre, therefore, on 4.1, 6.1 (but less so), and 9.1, as well as on whether there are exactly ten main units. For example, with the sharp changes of subject at 3.3 and 3.9 can the whole of chap. 3 be seen as a single unit? Coote (1981: 66) ends the first unit at 3.8 rather than 2.16. An important point here is that where there is no introductory formula at all, as at 3.3 or 3.9, or 5.21, it seems doubtful that the editor intended a strong break. Many scholars would place the next main break after 3.1 at 4.4 rather than 4.1, especially on the grounds that like 3.9-15, 4.1-3 targets Samaria (e.g. Jeremias 1998: 56-57). Möller replies that both chap. 3 and chap. 4 include references to Bethel as well as Samaria, so this is not a decisive issue (Möller 2003: 95).

Amos 9.1-6 (and therefore 8.4-14) may also be included in a vision sequence beginning at 7.1, and 9.7 seen as starting a new unit (Andersen and Freedman 1989; Jeremias 1998). In this case the sequence is interrupted twice, and it is certainly interrupted at least once. It can be argued that 7.10-17 is simply attached to 7.9 (seen as part of Yhwh's words in the vision) because of Amaziah's similar quotation from Amos in v. 11. Or it may illustrate the blind refusal of the people to accept that Amos's message is from Yhwh at just the point when Yhwh's patience runs out (Möller 2003: 135-36). It is more difficult to account for 8.4-14 being included in the vision sequence, as 8.4-6 reverts to the kind of satire seen earlier in the book. Möller, who does not take 9.1-6 as part of the unit beginning in 7.1, may be right in suggesting that at 8.4 Amos is shown as beginning the argument again 'one last time', even at the eleventh hour.

It seems to me that on the whole Möller's sectioning of the book is convincing, but he does not see it as a series of rigid divisions, and we should not take it that way. For example, 3.2 certainly looks back to 1.3–2.16 as well as forward to 3.11-15: 'you only have I known *of all the families of the earth*'—and yet their punishment also has been set out in some detail.

However, the identification of sections by opening formulas does not in itself show that such sections are true rhetorical units, that is, passages with a continuous argument, rather than small anthologies. It is largely the aim of Möller's book to show how they, and the whole book, can be seen as such. To examine every unit from this point of view is beyond the scope of this book, but the next chapter discusses a number of basic questions about the movement of thought of the book as a whole.

Further Reading

Karl Möller's *A Prophet in Debate* (Möller 2003) includes by far the most thorough recent study of the numerous proposals for the structure of the book of Amos, as well as setting out his own. But most commentaries make some attempt to set out the structure of the book: contrasting proposals may be studied in those of Andersen and Freedman (1989: 9-18) and of Jeremias (1998: 5-9).

For samples of how comprehensively Amos can be read as a chiasm, or a series of them, the most accessible sources are probably P.R. Noble's 'The Literary Structure of Amos's (Noble 1995) and the chapter on Amos in David Dorsey's *The Literary Structure of the Old Testament* (Dorsey 1999). But Jan de Waard's seminal work on Amos 5.1-17 (de Waard 1977) is also easily accessible, and short.

Chapter 3

The Aim of the Book of Amos

'The end has come upon my people Israel' (8.2). The main theme of the book of Amos is clear to every reader. The studies we have already carried out in the previous two chapters have only served to reinforce first impressions. The nation of Israel (that is, the northern kingdom with its capital at Samaria) is subject to the judgment of God, primarily for social injustice, and is due for destruction. However, there are issues raised by the way in which this theme is developed that need to be discussed. Even the simple sentence just quoted has a number of ambiguities. What is meant by 'the end'? What precisely is meant by 'Israel'?

Is it possible to trace a continuous argument or movement of thought in the book? In particular, is the upbeat conclusion in any way coherent with the prophecies of judgment that have gone before? Who precisely are Amos's judgment speeches aimed at, the nation as a whole or only those who are identified as oppressors? Can he be seen as responding to their objections? Most difficult of all, what is his strategy? Is he trying to persuade the Israelites that they are in great danger, calling on them to repent and change their behaviour to avoid disaster? Or is he simply announcing that, the time for repentance being past, they must 'prepare to meet your God'?

Movement of Thought

This is not an issue that exercises most commentators, who are largely dominated by the view of the prophetic books as collections of short texts; even those who base their comments on larger rhetorical units do not necessarily trace an argument right through the book. Commentators may see the book as offering a *consistent* message, but not usually as developing it continuously from chapter to chapter. However, there are two examples of such a view that we may glance at; but it will be impossible to test their views in the limited space available, as the only effective test is to follow the argument right through the book.

Coote, who interprets the main substance of the present book (1.1–9.6) as composed in the late seventh century in Judah (see below, p. 77), divides the book into three blocks. The first block, 1.3–3.8, looks to the past: it recalls Yhwh's threats against the nations, including Israel, that have been fulfilled. The second and third blocks, from 3.9 to 9.6, are directly addressed to the book's present audience, and offer an open future: Yhwh will destroy them also unless they obey the prophet and turn to him. They warn the survivors of Israel to cease worshipping at Bethel, which will be destroyed, and therefore to come to Jerusalem. At the same time, by the inclusion of Amos's eighth-century oracles in the structure, the Jerusalem elite is warned to avoid the fate of those of Samaria.

Möller also understands the book to be looking back on the ministry of Amos from a Judaean base, though he thinks it was composed not long after Amos left the scene (Möller 2003: 109). He describes the book, as his title suggests, as presenting Amos in debate with his audience. It tries 'to persuade its hearers or readers to learn from the failure of the prophet's audience to respond appropriately to the message' (Möller 2003: 122). So he sets out to describe 'the debate as it unfolds throughout the book' (125-47). This is difficult to summarize, and I can only suggest that you read it.

The contention that many of the utterances in Amos are responses to objections was not new with Möller; it is an important theme in Wolff 1977 and Jeremias 1998, and the point is reasonably convincing. I cite a few examples. The first is 3.2: the people will have objected that as they are Yhwh's people, he would not punish them, and Amos replies that for that very reason they are acountable to him. The saying in 9.7 is very similar. Clearly 3.3-8 is a reply to people who are questioning Amos's authority, and Amos in 7.14-15 makes a similar point, this time to the explicit rejection of his message by Amaziah. Amos's 'woe' against 'you who long for the day of Yhwh' (5.18) may well answer an objection relying on a national tradition like 3.2 and 9.7.

Nevertheless, Möller's contention that the book presents a debate between Amos and his audience is not entirely convincing. Long stretches are simply monologues by Amos. That he has a stubborn and unconvinced audience in his sights throughout may be granted, but he is only occasionally responding to what they are saying. Nor is it clear that there is a continuous thread of argument throughout; the 'debate' returns repeatedly to the same point.

Möller is on safer ground in commenting on the rising tension through the book, and certainly in seeing 9.1-4 and its sequel as the climax of the judgment theme of the book (2003: 138). There is 'a growing sense of natural and supenatural menace' until in the visions 'the menace is immediate and life-threatening' (Mills 2010: 170). All three of the major formulaic series move towards a climax, and each climax is on a higher note than the previous one: 'I will not revoke the punishment'... 'prepare to meet your God'... 'not one of them shall flee away, not one of them shall escape.'

There is also a rising curve in the specific disasters forecast. In 2.13-16 it is defeat in battle; in 3.11-15 siege and destruction; in 4.3 for the first time exile, which is repeated several times in the remainder of the book; in 5.16, 6.9-10 and 8.10 mass deaths; in 6.14 invasion and occupation; in 8.8 and 9.1 a devastating earthquake. The whole book is clearly arranged to lead up to the final rejection of Israel and destruction of Yhwh's enemies. My conclusion would be that although a continuous *argument* is not demonstrable, there is a clear structure to the prophecy presented, which leads the reader onward to the grim finale—except that it is not the finale! The so-called 'epilogue' (9.8 or 9.11 to 9.15) is discussed below.

Who is the Prophecy of Judgment aimed at?

Those who are denounced as sinners in the oracles of judgment, where they can be identified, are invariably of the ruling class or at least well-to-do, and their victims are the poor. Normally in these oracles, as one might expect, it is the evildoers themselves who are to be punished. The one apparent exception to this is 2.6-16. Although in vv. 6b-8 there is a clear division between culprits and victims, the oracle as such appears to address the nation as a whole, as in v. 6a and 9-12; the punishment in vv. 14-16 is the defeat of the entire army (v. 13 is obscure).

More importantly, there are many passages where doom is pronounced simply on 'Israel' (or 'Joseph' or 'Jacob'): besides 2.6, there are 3.1-2, 14; 4.12; 5.1-2, 6, 15, 25-27; 6.14; 8.2; 9.7. At 9.8-10 a distinction appears to be drawn. The house of Jacob will not be completely destroyed. It is only 'the sinners of my people' who will be killed. But it is doubtful whether v. 10 really draws a distinction: it may simply mean 'all those Israelite sinners' (see Noble 1997: 337; Garrett 2008: 280; Hadjiev 2009: 118; and on the other side Timmer 2014: 108 n. 18).

A number of different resolutions of this contradiction have been offered. Some rely on distinguishing earlier and later layers of the text (e.g. Coote 1981): it is the historical Amos who denounces oppressors, and the judgment is expanded to the entire nation at a later stage. See Chapter 7.

But taking the book as it stands, we may note two very different approaches. Daniel Carroll Rodas argues from the passages attacking or satirizing worship at the pilgrimage shrines (4.4-5; 5.4-5, 21-27; 7.9, etc.). The cult offered a world-view sanctioning oppression and therefore opposed to Yhwh's will, and Israel was involved in it as a whole, therefore they all shared in the guilt of the ruling class who organized it (Carroll R. 1992: 205; 209-10, 219, 273-77; Noble 1997). But it is very doubtful that the people as a whole, including the poorest, participated in the worship at the state temples and pilgrimage shrines (Bethel, Gilgal, Beersheba). To leave one's work for several days to travel to the temple and share in a week-long

festival would be beyond the resources of the poor people who figure as victims in Amos (Houston 2008: 55). Amos and the editors of his book would
be well aware of this. These passages do not justify extending the judgment
to the whole of Israel.

The other, more widespread, approach takes the passages that specify the
state and its institutions as the targets of attack as the key to understanding
the prophecy as a whole. Haroldo Reimer (1992) points to 7.9, which shows
that it is the monarchy and its cult sites that are to be destroyed, and this is
what is meant by 'my people Israel' in the previous verse. Möller (2003:
139-41, 145) takes 9.8-10 as the key passage, which nuances such a text as
8.2: it is the sinful *kingdom* that is to be destroyed, and after sifting, all the
sinners of my people are to be killed—and the sinners are closely identified
with the kingdom: they are the ruling class and its hangers-on. That is what
is meant by 'the end of my people Israel'; and rhetorical exaggeration also
needs to be taken into account. See also Hayes 1988: 221.

It is unreasonable to take 'the end has come upon my people Israel' (8.2),
or 'not one of them shall escape' in 9.1, as meaning that every single person
in the nation is to die (as Noble solemnly argues, 1997: 338). Koch (1982:
44) points out that several texts assume there will be people left after 'the
end' (5.16-17; 6.14; 8.3). Certainly 9.1 targets particular people, the power
groups attacked throughout the book; and 'the end for my people Israel' is
the end of their organized state.

However, besides the dubious interpretation of 9.10 relied on here, such
texts as 4.6-12; 5.3; 6.9-10 imply the deaths of many far beyond the ranks
of the oppressive elite. And as I have argued elsewhere, it is not true that the
poor, largely peasants, would be likely to escape the effects of an invasion
(let alone an earthquake: 4.11; 8.8; 9.1, 5-6; cf. Marlow 2009: 150). Invading armies lived off the land, and what they did not steal of the peasants'
crops, they burned. There is no way in which death and destruction could
realistically be confined to a select few. 'The threat of war as judgment is
a threat levelled at the whole of society' (Houston 2008: 60; cf. Houston
2010b: 52-54; Barton 2012: 124). Amos's denunciations may only target
an elite, but the judgment involves everyone. His expectations of the future
are entirely realistic, but understood as the deliberate judgment of God they
raise a serious moral problem. This is considered below (see pp. 47-48).

Inexorable Doom?

The question whether prophetic judgment oracles, taken in their context,
announce and justify inescapable destruction, or are warnings giving people
the opportunity to repent and be saved, applies to all the prophets of judgment, not only Amos, so it has been widely discussed. But it is particularly
in Amos that we find oracles pronouncing seemingly inescapable doom side

by side with exhortations that suggest an open future. Amos 5.1-17 is the classic example (see above, p. 22). Here, 'perhaps Yhwh, the God of hosts, will take pity on the remnant of Joseph' (5.15) is immediately followed by 'in all the squares there will be mourning' (5.16). This makes the contrast unbearably stark.

Again, the question is which of a number of apparently conflicting texts should be taken as the key to the rest. Most recent commentators take texts like 'the end has come upon my people Israel' as the key. Texts of warning or exhortation, such as 5.6, 'Seek Yhwh and live!' are explained in various ways. Wolff, for example, sees 5.4-5 as a word of Amos taking up an objection from a hearer, that Yhwh promised life, and turning it into part of his prophecy of death, 'Gilgal shall go into exile, and Bethel shall come to nothing'; 5.6 and 14-15 are then later interpretations of 5.4 with a different meaning (Wolff 1977: 237-40, 250-51). Coote (1981), similarly, assigns the judgment oracles to Amos and material leaving the future open to his later editors. A.V. Hunter (1982: 56-113) explains all these exhortations as ironical subversions of assurances that hearers might have been accustomed to hear in the cult. In 5.14-15 the exhortation to hate evil and love good in order to establish justice is meant seriously, but by slipping in 'perhaps' before the assurance of mercy Amos pulls away the guarantee of salvation. This is entirely compatible with his message of judgment (Hunter 1982: 98).

Barton argues in several articles (especially 1990, 2009) that the classical prophets, including Amos, began with the persuasion of disaster and then justified it by finding sins that could account for it; in other words their oracles are a theodicy.

> The genius of the classical prophets was to take the highly recalcitrant facts of history, whose religious and moral implications were in fact extremely ambiguous, and to give an account of these facts which would convince people not only that the hand of God could be seen in them, but that the operations of the divine hand were entirely comprehensible in human moral categories (Barton 1989: 52).

This reading fits the vision series in Amos very well; but the rhetoric of the rest of the book puts things the other way round (Koch 1982: 43).

The opposing viewpoint is that prophecies of judgment, however unconditional, are in reality intended to awaken the hearers to the imminent danger and induce a change of heart. Möller's general characterization of the book of Amos (2003: 122), that 'it is best understood as an attempt to persuade its hearers or readers to learn from the failure of the prophet's audience to respond appropriately to his message', implies that, in the book, the prophet does expect a response, in other words that his words are persuasive rather than simply condemnatory.

An alternative approach, urged especially by G.F. Hasel (Hasel 1972: 199-207; followed by Paul 1991: 178), argues that Amos allows for a repentant converted remnant, the 'remnant of Joseph' (5.15), to remain after judgment has been executed on the majority. This remnant consists of those who have 'responded appropriately' to Amos's message. However, it seems more likely that 'the remnant of Joseph' is simply the rump of the kingdom that is left after invaders, or rival claimants to the throne, have occupied most of it (Hayes 1988: 167; Jeremias 1998: 96).

I have argued (Houston 1993, esp. 182-87; cf. Zenger 1988) that while it is impossible to guess the intentions of the original speakers of prophecies of judgment, they were not simply 'stating a fact', nor were they merely giving a warning. They were declarative acts akin to a judicial sentence: they placed the offenders under judgment. Coote asserts that Amos's words were 'of no use' to his hearers (1981: 42). But a range of examples shows that an accepted response to such a declaration was one of mourning and prayer, suggesting the possible *alternative* fates of death and of forgiveness (see, e.g. 1 Kgs 21.27; 2 Sam. 12.16-17; Jonah 3). Some prophecies, such as Amos 2.6a (and all the preceding oracles against the nations), specifically exclude the possibility of forgiveness: but this suggests that 'revoking the punishment' was a possibility in principle, even if excluded in these cases. The different possibilities have been realized when such prophecies have been applied to new situations (see Chapter 8).

However, the movement of the prophecy through the book of Amos, as we saw it above, works to close down the possibility of forgiveness, even if it is initially open; this is clear above all in the visions sequence. I emphasize this because Möller (2001: 365-71; 2003: 142-45) has drawn on my article to argue that these prophecies may have been intended as warnings. But in fact we cannot tell this. All we can tell is how they work in the context of the book; and that is ultimately to face the people with their 'end'.

In the technical vocabulary of rhetoric (see Möller 2003: 39-40), Amos's prophecy is an example of *judicial* rhetoric, which would aim to persuade the hearers of a fact, that they were offenders in the eyes of God and would justly undergo his punishment. Möller suggests, however, that the purpose of the book's editors is *deliberative*—that it aims to persuade the hearers of the book to *do* something. There would still be a judicial aim: to persuade them that Israel's fate was just; but also a deliberative one: that they ought, by acting rightly, to avoid the same fate.

How does the Epilogue fit?

'Roses and lavender instead of blood and iron.' Thus Wellhausen (1967: 96) with laconic sarcasm dismisses 9.13-15 as having anything to do with Amos; but he also thinks none of 9.8-15 can be his work, and in this he has been followed by the great majority of critical scholars (except sometimes for v. 8a). We shall look at that issue in Chapter 7 (pp. 74, 76), but here we have a different question: not whether any of these words (there are probably three distinct oracles: 8-10, 11-12 and 13-15) go back to Amos, but whether they can be seen as a convincing conclusion to the *written prophecy* of Amos as a rhetorical unity. The last two are marked off from the body of the prophecy, which announces imminent judgment, by phrases that push their fulfilment into the indefinite future: 'on that day' (9.11); 'behold, days are coming' (9.13).

Jeremias (1998: 160-70) interprets them (with v. 7) as reflecting discussions about the meaning of Amos's words. Verse 7 responds to an objection in a similar way to 3.1-2, while vv. 8-10 reflect on the vision in 9.1-4 in a situation where both 'sinful kingdoms' have already been destroyed, and try to answer the question, 'To whom do Amos's words still apply?' The 'booth of David' to be re-erected in v. 11 will not be a 'sinful kingdom' but one open to the prophetic word, and therefore it will be possible for 'my people Israel' to be re-established on its land.

Möller (2003: 145-47) argues for a smooth connection with the rest of the book on the level of the prophecy as well as the book. There is a glimmer of hope, and this hope 'encourages those who are not to be counted among the ["sinners of my people" (Hebrew in Möller)] by pointing beyond the divine judgment to a time when Israel's fortune will be restored. But, at the same time, it is also an attempt to motivate the audience to change their lifestyle, indicating what they would have to gain by not being part of the ["sinners of my people"]' (146). Barton (2012: 98-99) also tentatively suggests, with a reference to the penitential psalms, that the theodicy of the book, showing that Yhwh's judgment is just (cf. Ps. 51.4), could also imply the possibility that on the other side of disaster there may be a future (cf. Ps. 51.10-12). This interpretation relies on an interpretation of v. 10a that we have noted as being dubious, and even so how convincing it is depends on the question we discussed above, whether Amos's judgment prophecy is aimed at conversion. In any case, how could v. 11, with its reference to the 'booth of David', meaning probably the dynasty of David ruling in Jerusalem, motivate an audience in the kingdom of Israel who rejected Davidic rule, or considered Judah a mere vassal kingdom?

It is reasonably obvious that v. 8b, 'however, I will certainly not destroy the house of Jacob', is intended as a correction to v. 8a (Hadjiev 2009: 115, as well as many commentaries). Some will escape: this points forward to vv. 13-15.

But vv. 9-10 does not share in this hope. Yhwh's 'shaking of Israel among all the nations' (v. 9) refers to its existence in diaspora (Rudolph 1971: 277; Garrett 2008: 279). Even in exile sinful Israel will not be able to escape their fate. Few scholars, however, interpret vv. 9-10 in this way, either deleting 'among all the nations' as a gloss (Cripps 1955: 266), or interpreting the metaphor of the sieve as implying a separation between 'sinners', who will be destroyed, and 'righteous' (not mentioned!), who will not.

Carroll R. (1995: 119-20) argues that in a literary reading of the book as a whole, the reader does not have to choose between the picture of judgment by war and the final picture of peace. They are held in tension. 'Indeed, the description of the utopia depends on the realities of the present and soon coming loss and makes no sense without them.'

It is possible to understand vv. 11-12 as appealing to a Judaean audience *of the completed book*, but hardly to the Israelite audience assumed by the prophecy in general. The same is true of the assurance of prosperity and rebuilding in 9.13-15. I conclude that vv. 11-15 are not a convincing conclusion to *the prophecy of Amos* as presented by the book, though they can be seen as an appropriate encouragement to hearers of the book as it now stands.

Further Reading

Möller 2003 asks and attempts to answer all the questions raised here. However, it is not an easy read for the student, as it uses Hebrew (in Hebrew characters) freely, and the works it refers to tend to be largely in German.

There is a brief discussion covering most of the issues in Houston 2008: 52-60.

Coote 1981 sets out what he perceives as the structure, setting and message of his 'B stage', which is effectively the book we now have, apart from the epilogue. It is very easy and even exciting to read.

Noble 1997 argues with specific reference to 9.1-10 that the entire nation is to die, 'down to the very last person'.

On the question of doom or warning, a lot has been written. Barton has a lucid discussion (2012: 92-103). Möller (2003: 141-42) gives a large number of references in nn. 121, 122, 123, but they are almost all in German. His own discussion is brief (141-45). For the opposing view, see Westermann 1967: 16-21 and Wolff 1977: 102-104. Hunter 1982 is a doctoral thesis that is rather hard going. Houston 1993 is I hope much less so, though it is largely taken up with an exposition of the theory of speech acts.

On the epilogue, see the good brief discussion by Hadjiev (2009: 111-23).

Chapter 4

THE ETHICAL IDEAS OF THE BOOK OF AMOS

The acts of judgment announced by Amos are based on accusations of wrongdoing. Such accusations imply ideas of right and wrong, in other words ethical ideas. How may we analyse these ideas and, if possible, demonstrate their coherence?

Much that has been written about the ethics of Amos, or the prophets in general, is not concerned with such analysis, but rather with the question of where Amos (or his editors) got his moral ideas. It has been argued at different times that Amos is dependent on the law, as expressed in the so-called Covenant Code (Exod. 20.23–23.33), or on wisdom, exemplified in Proverbs. These are important questions, and I shall briefly examine them (pp. 40-41). But they are not strictly ethical questions. Ethical questions are such as 'What is the good, or the right thing to do?', or 'How can we know what is good?' In the case of Amos, I am asking, 'What is the moral ideal (or ideals) expressed or implied by the accusations (and exhortations) in the book of Amos?'; 'What does Amos see as wrong in the types of behaviour that he denounces?'; and 'How should the people denounced have known that they were doing wrong?'

The Social Context of Ethics

Ethical ideas in any society are closely related to its structure and customs. In Chapter 6 we shall investigate what we can know of the social background of the writing of the book. But we cannot avoid anticipating that discussion to some extent here in our reading of the book to show how, conversely, its ethics imply a particular kind of society, the society that Amos is presented as addressing in his prophecy.

In the first place, it appears plainly as a society divided along class lines. The victims of injustice are almost uniformly described as poor. However, widows, fatherless children and resident aliens, the trio that appears frequently elsewhere as vulnerable and deserving of compassion, are not once referred to in Amos (and the alien never in the eighth-century prophets). Three different words for 'poor' are used: *dal*, *'ebyôn* and *'ānî*. They seem to be used interchangeably by Amos (Schwantes 1977: 99), although some have sought to make careful distinctions between them: most commonly it is thought that *dal* refers to a person with some little property, while *'ebyôn* refers to one who is destitute or reliant on casual employment, and *'ānî* connotes a state of miserable poverty in need of help (Fleischer 1975: 279; see these words in *NIDOTTE*).

The perpetrators are not similarly described as rich, but the details that emerge about them suggest that they belong to an upper-class stratum that is both rich and powerful. This is implied by the frequent reference to Samaria, the capital (3.9; 4.1; 6.1), as their place of residence, as also by the luxury of their houses (3.15) and their ritual meals (6.4-6). Their power is implied in several places by their ability to ensure the outcome of legal processes (2.6, 8; 5.12), as well as of course by the mere fact that they are able to exploit the poor (e.g. 4.1).

While this division between rich and poor has often been explained as a division between city and village (see pp. 60-61), it should be noted that the only evidence for this in the text is the reference to a 'levy of grain' in 5.11. In 8.4-6, on the other hand, which speaks of the fraudulent sale of grain, the victims are surely city-dwellers, since grain is grown in the country and sold in the city.

The text yields a few more details about the way in which class division expresses itself in this society. It is a safe deduction from 2.6 and 8.6 (with the support of other texts, e.g. Neh. 5.1-5) that debtors or their family members can be enslaved, or to be more precise, can be made to work to discharge their debts. There may well be a further implication in 2.6 that such bonded workers can be sold into permanent slavery. This, with the other accusations, suggests that measures taken by the perpetrators to secure their own interests are leading to a deepening of the existing class divisions. There is no criticism of the division of society in itself in Amos: it must be the hardening of divisions and the intensification of exploitation that has called forth the prophet's protests (cf. Houston 2004).

Secondly, the text gives the impression that this is a society in which religious observance has a high profile. The type of observance that is referred to is pilgrimage to temples, especially Bethel, the principal state sanctuary (7.13), at the time of major festivals: 4.4-5; 5.5-6, 21-25; 9.1. Carroll R. (1992: 181; 205; 209-10, 219, 273-77) points out that religion in every society functions to legitimize the way that society constructs and understands its world so that the '[so-called] "natural order of things" appears as a divine given and mandate' (181). The cultic activities at Bethel served to legitimize the monarchy and its state apparatus. They may therefore, Carroll R. argues, validate the oppression which was an integral part of Israel's world. To participate in the cult is to share in maintaining a corrupt and unjust system, and Carroll holds that everyone in Israel is indicted for this: 'for so you love to do, *people* [lit. 'sons'] *of Israel*' (4.5: Carroll R. 1992: 209-10).

I have expressed reservations about the idea that everyone participated in the state cult above (pp. 27-28). The people criticized for their misdirected devotion are most probably the same as are criticized for oppression: the Samaria-based ruling class. I would also argue against the idea that the cult legitimizes oppression and corruption, or would be seen to do so. The image of the people and its ruling institutions presented in the cult will be an ideal, morally unimpeachable (see Houston 2008: 135-53 for an example). Oppression and injustice will not be part of the world view that the cult makes acceptable.

'Justice and righteousness'

It is not difficult to see a positive moral ideal expressed repeatedly in the same words in Amos 5–6:

> 'Those who turn justice into wormwood, and throw righteousness down to the ground' (5.7).

> 'You have turned justice into poison, and the fruit of righteousness into wormwood' (6.12). ('Wormwood' [*Artemisia*] is a bitter plant.)

> 'Let justice roll like water, and righteousness like an unfailing stream' (5.24).

Also, 'justice' occurs once on its own:

> 'Hate evil, love good, and establish justice in the gate' (5.15).

The translations 'justice' for *mišpāṭ* and 'righteousness' for *ṣᵉdāqâ* are conventional. Each word has a wide range of meaning, and these translations do not immediately convey the meaning of either in context, and especially not the sense expressed by the two words when they occur together. The combination often refers roughly to what we call 'social justice' (Miranda 1977: 93; Weinfeld 1992; 1995: 25-44). This is clear enough in Amos from the evils that are denounced, assuming that 'justice and righteousness' are the corresponding good.

The phrase is a hendiadys, expressing one idea in two words. Each of the words makes more precise the meaning of the other. *mišpāṭ* may mean rule, judgment, justice, custom, law, legal decision and more: linking it with *ṣᵉdāqâ* makes it clear it is a question of *just* rule, laws or customs. *ṣᵉdāqâ*'s range of meaning is even wider, covering right order, just conduct, generosity, prosperity, salvation, victory, to name a few of its connotations: but paired with *mišpāṭ* it is narrowed down to the sphere of social and political relationships. Taken together, they refer to God's just ordering of the world, and in the human realm to just and generous social and political relationships, or what we would call social justice, and the legal, political and religious means by which they may be ensured. Where *mišpāṭ* occurs alone in Amos 5.15, it should naturally be interpreted along the same lines, as justice in legal practice; but the hendiadys has a broader reference, to decrees of the ruler and conduct in society, as well as just judgment. Psalm 72, and Deut. 33.21, show that this justice is the gift of God, who both exercises it himself and enables his king and people to exercise it. For Koch (1982: 56-62), *mišpāṭ* and *ṣᵉdāqâ* are 'spheres of power', supernatural powers in the form of 'fluids' that pour down from Yhwh, and are received by people at the festivals to be exercised in practice. But in Amos they obstruct them, rather than letting them flow like water.

Analysing Injustice

These limited references to a positive moral ideal are the reverse side of the constant concern in Amos about injustice to the poor. In many cases, it is difficult to know precisely what the practice is that is condemned, as the references are brief and allusive, but what is wrong with it is never in doubt.

The test of social justice for Amos is the way in which the poor are treated. Apart from the words for 'poor' referred to above, Amos uses 'the righteous person' (*ṣaddîq*) twice (2.6; 5.12) and also 'the girl' (or young woman, Heb. *naᵃrâ*) in 2.7. Except for this last word, the words are always in the masculine. Although it is true that masculine words often include both sexes, Phyllis Bird argues persuasively that the concern is for poor *men* (Bird 1997; Houston 2008: 62-63). This does not mean that there is no concern for women and children; but they are seen as part of a man's family. It is significant that the very first word that is used for the victim of oppression is *ṣaddîq*, meaning, not necessarily a person of good morals, but 'innocent' in the circumstances, legally or morally, or a person *with rights* (Bendor 1996: 246). The central concern is not so much for physical privation as for the honour of poor but respectable members of society who are being dishonoured by their brutal treatment.

The way in which those guilty of injustice are referred to is quite different. No word indicates their dominant role in the state or society (contrast, e.g., 'elders and officers' in Isa. 3.14). Rather, they tend to be introduced or addressed by their *actions*: for example, 'because they sell...' (2.6), 'you who turn...' (5.7). Thus they are given no role or dignity beyond their treatment of the poor who are at their mercy.

That oppressive treatment can be described more precisely (Houston 2008: 60-69, 86-93). It consists first in *violence and coercion*. The Hebrew word *ḥāmās*, which is usually translated 'violence', though its meaning is rather broader, occurs at Amos 3.10, linked with *šōd*, 'robbery, rapine' in a common hendiadys 'implying violent, ruthless oppression and exploitation' (Houston 2008: 68). Amos also uses metaphors implying violence:

e.g. 'crushing the needy' (4.1), 'persecuting the righteous' (5.12; translation after Paul 1991: 157), and the word of disputed meaning in 2.7 and 8.4,
haššō'ᵃpîm. This I take to connote 'hunting down' (see Garrett 2008: 58-59;
Fleischer 1989: 30, 57-58), though some translators (e.g. NRSV) take it as
'trampling'. No doubt these descriptions are metaphorical, but in using violent metaphors the text expresses the understanding that there is hidden violence in all coercive actions. Coercion may sometimes be necessary for the
good of society, as when a criminal is arrested. But these actions are solely
for the benefit of those who perform them.

Secondly, there is *exploitation* or *extortion*, expressed characteristically
with the verb *'āšaq* (4.1: 'exploiting the poor') and related nouns (3.9). The
verb is often used along with the verb *gāzal*, 'rob', and it connotes obtain-
ing property or profit by extortion, by the use of superior power. Such gains
may be justified by some legal title, but the text is not interested in such
justifications; 'no matter how legal, the squeezing out of surplus product
is immoral' (Houston 2008: 69). It is indeed equivalent to robbery. And
elsewhere we find the motivation for oppression seen as financial: 'selling
the righteous for silver' (2.6); 'they take a levy of grain' (5.11); 'taking a
bribe' (5.12); and the whole passage on the corn-dealers (8.4-6). The way
in which such immoral gains might be used is portrayed satirically in 4.1b
and in 6.4-6.

Thirdly, while some gains are obtained by the use of power, others are
got by *dishonesty*, most obviously by the crooked corn-dealers in 8.5-6; the
phrase 'fraudulent scales' in 8.6 includes the specifically moral term *mirmâ*,
'fraud, treachery'. In 5.10 also, the point may be that advocates for the
accused are 'hated' because they expose the lies of the prosecutors.

Fourthly, the effect of these actions is portrayed from the point of view
of the victims as *depriving* them of their *rights* or *freedom* or *way of life*.
The poor are 'pushed out of the way' in their plea for justice (5.12). Amos
2.7aβ, 'they turn aside the way of the poor' may mean the same thing, but
Koch (1982: 46) interprets 'way' (Heb. *derek*) as the conditions of prosperous and harmonious life, in freedom on their own land. In 2.6 the 'selling'
of the poor—the first accusation against Israel—may refer to creditors' selling on into permanent slavery debt-slaves that they have acquired by fore-
closing on debts (Fleischer 1989: 50-53; cf. Jeremias 1998: 36-37). There is
no protest against the institution of debt-bondage in itself in Amos, unless
'buying the poor' in 8.6 is such. It was a means of saving a family from des-
titution and perhaps enabling one of their members to make a new start (see
Exod. 21.2-6; Deut. 15.12-18). But if 2.6 does not refer to selling a person
on to a third party, 2.6bα (selling *an innocent man* for silver) may attack the
forcing of someone into bondage without due cause, and 2.6bβ (a poor man
for a pair of sandals) foreclosure where the remaining sum owed is triv-
ial (Fleischer 1989: 47-57). (An alternative interpretation of 2.6b is that it

refers to depriving people of justice for a bribe.) Any of these abuses would have the effect of degrading a free member of the community to the status of a slave, either without good cause, or for life, or both. It should be noted, however, that in Amos, unlike Micah and Isaiah, nothing is said about the seizure of land (see further below, p. 63).

The actions of the oppressors are thus exposed as theft, robbery, violence and perversion of justice, backed up by bribery and dishonesty, and leading to the degradation of their victims. They are not portrayed as transgressors against some law, nor as destroying some ideal state of society, but simply as immoral, violating norms of human behaviour that have been accepted everywhere and at all times. Of course, that does not mean that *they* would have accepted that their treatment of the poor could be described in that way, or that it was as blameworthy as the war crimes denounced in the oracles against the nations (Barton 2012: 60; Houston 2008: 93). They would doubtless have argued for its legality and necessity. But it does mean that they knew the norms against which they were being judged, and that the victims, for whom Amos speaks, would certainly see that they had violated them. No new morality is being propounded.

However, Amos applies these universally accepted norms not just to the behaviour of individuals but to the relations between classes and to characterize the polity as a whole, so that he can be described as an advocate of *social* justice. None the less, there is nothing that can be described as social analysis, as we would understand it. Still less can we view Amos as a social reformer. 'Hate evil and love good, and establish justice in the gate' (5.15) does not amount to a social programme, and you would hardly expect one in a book which announces the destruction of the state.

Justice between the Nations

The first six of the 'oracles against the nations' (1.3–2.3) are concerned with an entirely different subject. The offences of which these states surrounding Israel are accused would be described today as war crimes. They include brutality against civilians (1.3, 13: it is not clear precisely what the metaphor 'threshing with threshing sledges of iron' (v. 3) refers to, but it must be some act of violence); the selling of entire populations into slavery (1.6, 9); breach of treaty (1.9); and the treatment of the dead with indignity (2.1).

Unlike the acts condemned within Israel, it is not so clear that these are generally recognized and universally condemned acts of wrongdoing. As a rule, people apply a lower standard of morality to their interactions with foreigners than to those with their own people, and warfare in the ancient world was ruthless and generally lacking in rules or restraint. See Deut. 20.10-14 for the best that can be said about Israelite standards.

Barton (1980: 3-6, 46-47 [= 2003: 78-81, 115-16]; also 2012: 57-61) argues from the 'surprise' strategy of the oracles against the nations (see above, p. 18). The rhetorical strategy relies on the assumption that the hearers must have believed that God could be expected to punish such acts as these, and that the nations committing them ought to have known they were wrong; in other words, Israelites had some idea that there were certain acts that should not be done in warfare, a rudimentary idea of the laws of war. The instruction in Deuteronomy 20 confirms this; see also 1 Kgs 20.31. Although the rhetoric implies that the nations knew or should have known they were doing wrong, it does not follow that they actually did know. The evidence suggests that the belief that there are moral limits on how one should treat non-combatants or the land in war was distinctive of Israel. See Barton 1980: 51-61 (2003: 118-28).

Ethics and the Cult

The ironic and slighting words of Amos about the pilgrimage cult are difficult to analyse ethically. They do not occur in oracles of judgment, which are invariably concerned with acts of injustice. (But Bethel and other pilgrimage sites are warned of disaster.) However, they do imply an ethical position. In 4.4 Israelites are ironically invited to 'come to Bethel and *sin*', using the verb *pāša'*, related to the noun *peša'* used in the oracles against the nations, and in 5.21-3 Yhwh is said to 'hate' and 'despise' all their main acts of worship.

I have already contested Carroll R.'s view that the cult in itself served to legitimate injustice. However, the rejection of the cult is indeed based on the injustice of society. In 5.24 'justice and righteousness' are contrasted with worship. If the addressees stop trying to please Yhwh through sacrifice and hymn singing, then his gift of social justice will have a chance to flow. I suggest translating v. 24 'so that justice may roll like water', etc. (cf. Koch 1982: 57). In other words, worship for the Israelite elite is what psychologists call a displacement activity: they engage in it in order to avoid their true responsibility of doing justice for the poor (Wolff 1977: 219), or mistakenly believing that this, rather than justice, is Yhwh's desire for Israel.

This would suggest that the ethical principle involved is no different from that in the oracles of judgment. However, it has been frequently discussed whether the 'sin' was in offering (sacrificial) worship at all, in other words whether Amos and other prophets were absolutely and in principle opposed to sacrifice, pilgrimages and the temple cult with all its ritual. See Barton 2005 and 2012: 84-92 for characteristically clear discussions of the issue. But his conclusion, that Amos (with other prophets) envisaged a religion without ritual is inherently unlikely (Koch 1982: 55). Koch's suggestion that Amos envisages a ritual of repentance in place of a festival of rejoicing is perhaps equally unlikely.

Such plain assertions as Amos 5.24 or Mic. 6.8 make it clear that what is at stake is not a theory about religion, but the divine demand for justice. Amos's rejection of Israel's worship springs out of his central message. Israel's relationship with Yhwh is broken. It cannot be repaired by those cultic activities that are supposed to express it, and the cult is therefore pointless (Boecker 1981: 175). Its only function is to tickle the participants' own fancy: 'for so you love to do, people of Israel!' (4.5). The worshippers were pleasing themselves, not God.

There is a further and theologically more profound point, that emerges directly out of Yhwh's ironical 'Seek me, but do not seek Bethel' (5.4-5), especially as compared with the parallel text in 5.14-15 'Seek good and not evil... hate evil and love good, and establish justice in the gate'. To 'seek' God was a technical term meaning to attend worship or make an inquiry of priest or prophet. God is not to be *found* at the sanctuary, but in the practice of justice. Therefore in engaging in worship, Israelites were praising a god who was not actually there. 'Israel celebrates Yahweh as if its relationship with God were intact, utterly unaware that he is not even present at the celebration' (Jeremias 1998: 103; cf. Miranda 1977: 57-58).

The Ground of Ethics

In any ethical system, there will be, behind the individual precepts or ideas that this or that is right or wrong, an idea, perhaps unconscious, of the basis of morality in general.

There is a widespread assumption that Old Testament morality is based purely and simply on God's will, as expressed in the covenant laws of the Pentateuch. It was at one time, and still is among more conservative scholars, the accepted view that the condemnations of Israel and Israelites in Amos are for violation of the covenant with Yhwh as expressed in Exodus or Deuteronomy (see, for example, Mays 1969: 7; Paul 1991: 76; Sloane 2008: 76), and it has been argued that the accusations are specifically based on laws in Exodus (Würthwein 1950; Bach 1957). So von Rad 1965: 136: 'Amos tied his contemporaries down to the simple, obvious, literal sense of these commandments' (cf. Andersen and Freedman 1989: 308, 320). Yet on the very next page von Rad must modify this conception so far, in respect of 6.4-6, that what is missing is 'a quality of heart and mind...; the breach of particular commandments is certainly not in question.'

For the covenant see further in the next chapter, pp. 44-45. What of the idea that Amos's condemnations appeal to the laws of the Torah? Obviously, there is some relationship, for example, between the law in Exod. 22.26-27 and the accusation in Amos 2.8a, since the garments in the Amos text are taken as pledges for debt (or, as Paul argues (1991: 83-84), distrained for non-payment), and lain on, therefore presumably at night and possibly leaving the owner without a covering. There is some kind of common tradition. But neither here nor anywhere else does Amos either quote a law or accuse people of 'breaking the law'. The prophets are not interested in the law as such, but only in justice (Miranda 1977: 166-67). In any case, the laws in question, the so-called 'apodictic laws', are not really laws as we would understand 'law', but moral teaching (see Houston 2013: 59-60). 'Both the prophet and the "law" appeal to known norms of humane conduct, of "justice and righteousness", norms which are exemplified in the "apodictic law", but cannot be limited by it' (Houston 2008: 70-71).

Appeal to the laws must have difficulty with the oracles against the nations, since they were not revealed to foreign nations, but only to Israel. Although some (e.g. Polley 1989) have argued that the nations are indicted for treaty violation, the use of the word *peša‘*, 'transgression' here is moral rather than political ('rebellion'): it implies deliberate transgression of a known moral norm, and thus that despite not knowing any commandments of Yhwh the nations were bound to certain moral norms that they did know. The norms transgressed are (as Israelites believe) 'part of the common moral sense of all right-minded people' (Barton 1980: 43 [2003: 112-13]).

Barton develops this idea further, under the heading of 'natural law', that is, morality which is seen as inherent to the world and is recognized by all humanity (Barton 2003: 32-44, 48-50; 2014). In 6.12 we read 'Do horses run over rocks? Does one plough the sea with oxen? Yet you have turned justice to poison, and the fruit of righteousness to wormwood'. ('Plough the sea' depends on a widely accepted emendation of the Hebrew text.) Barton says (2012: 81) that this verse 'explicates what is wrong about wrongdoing'. Social injustice is *unnatural*. It is 'a cosmic nonsense' (Barton 2003: 38), a violation of the natural order of justice, which is maintained by the Creator. So Amos 'may not be appealing to *divine law* to back up his claims, but more to moral inclinations he thinks are (or ought to be) common to people just as human beings' (Barton 2012: 82).

It is a mistake, then, to ask what the 'source' of Amos's ethics is, whether in the law, or, as others have argued, in tribal wisdom (Wolff 1973). The *basis* of Amos's ethics is the universal, taken-for-granted moral beliefs that everyone accepted (and accepts), which are attested in the law, in wisdom and in prophecy, but none of these is the source of the others. It is reasonable to refer to this as 'natural law', provided that this is not understood as the fully-developed theory of, e.g. Thomas Aquinas. And clearly part of this belief, in Israel's case, is that Yhwh punishes violations of these norms.

Further Reading

In recent discussion, the running has been made by John Barton. See Barton 1980 (2003: 77-129) on the oracles against the nations; 2003: 32-44; 48-50 on 'natural law'; 2012: 77-84 on the condemnation of Israel; 2005 and 2012: 84-92 on the cult. See now also Barton 2014.

For detailed analysis of the condemnations of social injustice in Amos, see Houston 2008: 60-69, 86-93.

The question of the prophets', including Amos's, attitude to the cult has been frequently discussed. Carroll R. 1992 ties it most closely to the injustice of society. The view given above is finely expressed in Jeremias 1998: 101-105, while Barton 2005 argues for a prophetic 'religion without ritual'. Barstad 1984 expounds the generally rejected view that Amos was concerned with Israel's non-Yahwistic or syncretistic cults, like Hosea. Unfortunately the recent detailed study by Lafferty (2012) contains numerous errors and is not to be relied on.

The older view of the ground of Amos's ethics is briefly stated in von Rad 1965: 130-38, and maintained in Sloane 2008.

Chapter 5

THE THEOLOGY OF THE BOOK OF AMOS

My aim here is to sketch the understanding of God, and of God's activity and relationship to Israel, as implied in the composition taken as a whole. There may be a few odd sentences that do not fit the general outlook, and these will be ignored; but I am satisfied that regardless of whether particular parts go back to the historical prophet or not, the composition is essentially harmonious from a theological point of view.

God

There is only one God recognized by the book of Amos, invariably referred to by the name Yhwh, sometimes 'Yhwh God of hosts' (Heb. *'elōhê-(ha) ṣ^ebā'ôt*). (The use of *'elōhîm* [NRSV 'God'] in 4.11 is a special case: see Cripps 1955: 175; Wolff 1977: 222; Andersen and Freedman 1989: 443.) In the couple of places where other gods are mentioned (5.26; 8.14) they are obviously regarded as mere idols. And, evidently, this God has power over nature (see especially 4.13; 5.8; 9.5-6, the hymn fragments, but also e.g. 4.6-11; 7.1; 8.8-9) and all nations (1.3–2.16; 9.7); his power is thus not confined to Israel. Gowan (1998: 34) speaks of a 'practical monotheism'— a cautious expression reflecting the fact that there is no explicit statement of monotheism in the book. Barton speaks more precisely: in Amos Yhwh 'is in effect the God of a monotheistic system of thought. Amos does not mention or have room in his thinking for any other divinity' (Barton 2012: 103).

One could go further: the implication of the hymn fragments, which all end 'Yhwh (of hosts) is his name', is that Yhwh is being praised as the creator in contrast to any other god; but this is also implied in what is said about Yhwh's control of nature elsewhere. Yhwh is the creator: but he is also, and overwhelmingly in Amos, the destroyer, who uses both nature and human powers to inflict devastation on Israel and other nations (Barton 2012: 101; Marlow 2009: 146; Mills 2010).

Yhwh and Israel

The most disputed issue in the theology of Amos is the relation between Yhwh and Israel. In what sense is Yhwh the God of Israel? Yhwh is never called that in Amos; on the other hand, he is twice called 'your God' (4.12; 9.15), and four times calls Israel 'my people' (7.8; 8.2; 9.10, 14). Is Amos announcing a change in the relationship? Some argue that the basis for Yhwh's action in judgment in Amos is his special relationship to Israel, defined as 'election' (e.g. von Rad 1965: 133), and encapsulated in 3.2, or 'covenant' (e.g. Clements 1965; and see above, p. 40). Others point out that there is no difference between Yhwh's treatment of Israel and of other nations; 9.7 appears to suggest that any special relationship there may have been is at an end, or never existed, in which case 'a central pillar of Amos's theology may be called the *non-election of Israel by Yhwh*' (Barton 2012: 74, italics original).

Do 3.2 and 9.7 contradict each other (cf. Barton 2012: 73-74)? Formally they do: one says that Yhwh will punish Israel because there is an exclusive relationship between the two; the other says that Israel means no more to Yhwh than the distant Nubians (Cushites or 'Ethiopians' [NRSV]), and that Israel has no advantage in Yhwh's actions in the history of nations. But rhetorically they have the same effect: the intention of both verses is to deny that Israel can claim privilege with Yhwh because they are his people. It is unnecessary to pit the verses against each other, as Hadjiev does (2009: 30-31).

Yhwh is after all Israel's God. But what does this mean? The use of the expression 'election' is inaccurate, because this idea, of Yhwh's choosing Israel from among the nations, is distinctive of Deuteronomy, and the relationship is not expressed in this way in Amos. What 3.2 does say is that Israel is the only people that Yhwh recognizes or has dealings with; 2.9-11 (as well as 3.1 and 9.7) speak of what Yhwh has done for Israel, but it is not said that this is the basis of the relationship, as suggested by von Rad (1965: 133) and Clements (1965: 48-49). Clearly 3.2, in its context immediately after the oracles against the nations, cannot mean that it is *only* a nation in a special relationship that will be punished by Yhwh. It is very likely that 3.2 echoes an objection from Amos's hearers (Möller 2003: 125), and Yhwh's riposte is that that is all the more reason to 'hold them to account' (Paul's translation, 1991: 100, 102).

That the relationship is understood as formalized by a 'covenant' or treaty is still a widespread view. Paul, e.g., links the use of 'know' in 3.2 with the language of treaties (1990: 101-102); cf. Gowan 1998: 32-34. The view was set out clearly by Clements in 1965. It was generally believed in Israel that they had entered into a commitment at Sinai to obey the commandments of Yhwh, and on that condition enjoyed Yhwh's blessing. The prophets, including Amos, acted as (unofficial) spokesmen for the covenant (Clements 1965: 80), announcing that the nation as a whole had now effectively abandoned that commitment, and hence that Yhwh was justified in withdrawing from his side of the covenant.

That most scholars nowadays are unconvinced that the idea of the covenant was already current in the eighth century (see Nicholson 1986) is no objection to this, unless it could be shown that the book as a whole originated then, which the same scholars do not believe. The real objection is that the language of the accusations against Israel does not reflect the idea. Israel is not accused of breaking a covenant or laws, only Judah in 2.4, and then they are not specified. The accusations are simply of various modes of injustice, which would be wrong whoever was guilty of them. It is not true that in this respect 'Israel was supposed to be different' (Gowan 1998: 32). Injustice is injustice, whoever commits it. (See also above, pp. 40-41.)

A slightly different approach is taken by Barton (2012: 103-106), who does not think that the covenant idea was current in the eighth century, but rather that Amos originated it. Even though the terminology of covenant is not found in the book, his preaching as a whole implies a contractual relationship between Yhwh and Israel. Yhwh's continued relationship with them depends on their behaviour, and the behaviour of the ruling classes is particularly important for the fate of the nation as a whole. It is this sense of a contractual relationship that is eventually metaphorized as the striking of a treaty or 'covenant'. But even this idea seems not to meet the case, since the essence of a contract is mutual agreement, and there is no indication in Amos that the nation of Israel had agreed that Yhwh's protection should be conditional on their behaviour.

Yhwh's Action against Injustice

Nothing is more obvious in the book of Amos than that Yhwh punishes the guilty, and we have discussed basic questions about this above, pp. 27-32. What needs to be underlined here is the way it determines the characterization of Yhwh in the book. The aspect almost exclusively on view is that of Yhwh as the destroyer, who exercises violence against the violent. One passage (4.6-11) presents the destruction he brings as an act of discipline or warning, intended for Israel's good, to get them 'to return to me'. But in most of the rest of the book destruction is judgment, final punishment with no sequel. Only one passage again (7.1-6) presents Yhwh as relenting in his plan of destruction at Amos's plea. The emphatic refusal to relent displayed in the following three visions, as well as in the words of the oracles against the nations, 'I shall not turn it back', is the more salient characteristic of Yhwh as he appears in the book of Amos.

But this unrelenting determination to destroy is exercised, of course, against those guilty of injustice and violence. Walther Eichrodt, speaking of the prophets in general, uses the word 'wrath', but emphasizes that, unlike popular ancient ideas of divine wrath, this is not something arbitrary and irrational but is a response to sin (Eichrodt 1961: 259-60). Amos, as it happens, does not attribute 'wrath' or 'anger' to Yhwh. Judgment is carried out certainly by a personal God, rather than an impersonal force—'I shall not turn it back', 'I shall not pass them by', 'I shall not forget all their crimes'— yet without discernible passion, very unlike the passionate God of Hosea or Jeremiah.

God is thus represented as enforcing a moral equivalence between an act and its outcome for the actor. Sometimes the punishment visibly echoes the crime, as in 5.11—what is known as 'poetic justice' (cf. Barton 1979). Now the idea that the evil that you do will recoil on your own head is extremely widespread in the Old Testament, indeed in the Bible as a whole, and is constantly expressed in Proverbs, Psalms, and the prophets generally. Klaus Koch has even argued that there is no such thing as 'retribution' in the Hebrew Bible, but rather an automatic connection between act and consequence (Koch 1983). He could hardly assert this so simply as regards Amos, where Yhwh's responsibility for events is made so plain. But referring to 3.6, 'Does evil befall a city unless Yhwh has done it?', he argues that evil done by Yhwh 'signifies the absorption and implementation of human wickedness': in other words Yhwh simply steps in to hasten what would in any case be the inevitable consequence for people of their own wickedness (Koch 1982: 74). Koch has not convinced many scholars of the truth of this, but he has made a notable attempt to show the inner coherence of theologies in the Hebrew Bible that on the surface appear quite different.

How Yhwh Acts

In his visions, Amos has an extraordinarily vivid sense of the physical reality of Yhwh and his personal intervention in the life of Israel and the world. He sees Yhwh, though he never describes what he looks like (contrast, e.g. Ezekiel 1–3). But this direct physical involvement is not asserted in the oracles; here Yhwh is said to act through natural and human powers: fire (1.3–2.5), earthquake (3.14-15 possibly; 4.11; 8.8; 9.1, 5-6); and enemy armies (1.5; 3.11; 5.27; 6.7, 14; 7.17; 9.10 and elsewhere). For Koch (1982: 71), the (to us) abstract ideas of justice, righteousness and holiness should be added to the list.

But as Koch also rightly emphasizes, Yhwh acts first of all through his word spoken through the prophet. 'The Lord Yhwh has spoken: who will not prophesy?' (3.8). Koch says that Yhwh's word 'is an efficacious word' that 'realizes itself, even materializes, in the imminent future' (Koch 1982:

71). This relies on a view widespread at one time that words such as blessings and curses in the Hebrew Bible are real 'dynamic' entities that once spoken have automatic effects; Isa. 9.8 and 55.10-11, and Amos 7.10, are referred to in support.

This idea has been criticized by A.C. Thiselton (1974), who prefers to explain the sense that words do things by the idea, derived from J.L. Austin (1975), that such words are 'performatives', like the vows in a marriage service that create a marriage simply by being said in accordance with the law, not by magic. If that applies to a word of Yhwh's judgment spoken through the prophet, I have argued that it is because the word puts the addressee 'under judgment' and hence will be shortly followed by the execution of the sentence. The word does not physically accomplish that, but it does accomplish the condemnation of the culprits, which is judicially necessary (Houston 1993: 179-87 [=1995: 145-52]). I am less certain now that the process can be compared to a judicial one, but I would maintain that there is no sign in Amos of any autonomous power of the word. Amaziah's statement that 'the land cannot bear all his words' (7.10) has to be understood in the political context: he has just accused Amos to the king of conspiracy against him (Jeremias 1998: 138).

It might appear that seeing God as the agent setting events in motion is at odds with modern ideas of causality internal to the world: there are political processes that result in wars, and shifts in tectonic plates that cause earthquakes; the latter have nothing to do with injustice in human society, and while there may be a connection between injustice and war, it is to do with the interactions of human beings with free will rather than through an avenging God. This is perhaps to underestimate the subtlety of Hebrew thought: Koch at all events sees what he calls 'metahistory' in Amos as embracing all aspects of reality, divine, natural and human in a single complex process (Koch 1982: 73).

Does Yhwh Act Justly?

A problem arises when Yhwh punishes violations in a way that brings disaster not only on the perpetrators, but on the victims as well (see above, pp. 27-28). Doing justice in a situation of injustice should normally have two aspects: punishing (or converting) the oppressor, and more importantly delivering the oppressed and giving them new life. But the narrative of justice presented in Amos fails to achieve this, and instead subjects the victims to further misery. The last few verses of Amos have been read by some as offering a prosperous future to the rural people of Israel after being freed of their oppressors (e.g. Coote 1981: 121-27): but also after invading armies have consumed their crops and burnt their fields and houses! (Houston 2010b: 53).

It is entirely appropriate that the judgment on injustice in Israel should be the end of the state of Israel, since it is committed by representatives of the state and characterizes the state as such. But it is surely morally questionable that this takes place in a way that leads to indiscriminate death and destruction (Clines 1995: 90-92). Historically speaking, of course, this was inevitable, and is and always has been the effect of war. But according to this book it is not the impersonal forces of history but a personal god, Yhwh, with unlimited power and personal responsibility, who executes punishment.

The only way in which comprehensive disaster can be justified as punishment for the sins of a few is by the theory of corporate responsibility, today rejected in all civilized societies, that everyone in a group (originally a family, then a tribe or nation) shares the blame and the judgment for the crime of any member. This theory is clearly implicit in the prophecy of Amos (Barton 2012: 105-106; see Coote 1981 for a different view of Amos's original oracles). But, though widespread in the Hebrew Bible (see, e.g., Exod. 20.5; 34.7; Josh. 7.24-6), it is also questioned there, as in Gen. 18.23-32 or Ezekiel 18. There can be no *unthinking* resort to Amos in discussions of justice.

The Ultimate Purpose

One view of the popular belief in 'the day of Yhwh' (5.18) that Amos refers to is that it would be a day of final reckoning for Israel's enemies and final victory for Israel: an eschatological fulfilment, if eschatology is taken in a broad sense. If this is the idea that Amos challenges by asserting it will be a day of 'darkness, and not light', then for him the day of Yhwh will presumably be a day of final disaster for Israel, 'the end of my people Israel' (8.2), and the logical conclusion of the campaign of judgment announced by the prophet.

But this is to reckon without the 'epilogue'. Taking the book as a whole, it may be possible to see the eventual issue of judgment as being not the final extinction of the nation (not in any case every individual in it, see above, p. 28), but its making anew: 'I will not totally destroy the house of Jacob... they shall not again be plucked up from the land that I gave them' (9.8b, 15). It is clear, however, that the kingdom of Israel, the foundation of the first Jeroboam, will not be revived; the revived kingdom will be that of David (9.11). Barton (2012: 122-27) compares the message of this passage to that of many others in post-exilic prophets. The ultimate purpose of the divine judgment is not to destroy but to purify and renew.

And just as the God who has destroyed the kingdom of Israel will in due course act politically to revive the house of David, so the God who has set nature against Israel (4.6-11, 8.7-8) will in due course turn the powers of nature to bless them abundantly (9.13-15). It is unlikely that ancient writers and readers saw any difference between these two types of expectation, making one more miraculous than the other.

Further Reading

The only book-length study of the theology of the book of Amos, at least in English, is by Barton (2012), who surveys all the issues with his customary lucidity. Barton first of all deals with the historical-critical issues (see Section 7 here), and on the basis of his (quite conventional) results there looks separately at current Israelite ideas presupposed by Amos; the theology of the historical prophet Amos; that of the supposed additions to the book, and from various points of view that of the book understood as a composite work. His discussion of the covenant is to be found on pp. 103-106.

Other works that contain observations on the theology of Amos include von Rad 1965 (130-38), exemplifying an older approach; Koch 1982 (36-76), with his quite distinctive point of view; Gowan 1998 (25-37); and Marlow 2009 (120-57), who focuses on the role played by nature in the theology of the book.

The substantial current theologies of the Old Testament, other than von Rad's, do not have separate sections on Amos, but usually have treatments of prophecy that are relevant to Amos, as does von Rad. See, e.g., Eichrodt 1961: 338-91; von Rad 1965: 33-125; Brueggemann 1997: 622-49; Goldingay 2006.

Corporate responsibility is discussed in Kaminsky 1995, but with little attention to the prophets, other than Ezekiel.

Part II

WRITING AMOS

Chapter 6

THE CONTEXT OF THE MAKING OF THE BOOK OF AMOS

In this chapter we shall try to sketch the historical context in which the book of Amos came to be, in its political, religious, and social aspects, including any factors that have been considered relevant by significant scholars. We cannot confine ourselves to the period of time when Amos himself is said (in 1.1, cf. 7.9-11) to have been active, as most scholars have argued that the book took shape on a much longer timescale, reaching down as far as the Persian period (see Chapter 7). I shall not set out here a history of that relevant period. I assume that anyone reading this book will have at least a basic knowledge of the history of Israel and Judah. Instead, I shall tackle a selection of controversial issues, or ones on which new information is available, that are relevant, or have been thought relevant by some.

1. *General Historical Context*

The Reign of Jeroboam II

Most commentaries on Amos start by painting a picture of Israel in the reign of Jeroboam (roughly the first half of the eighth century—the precise dates of his 41-year reign are disputed): a prosperous, militarily successful, economically expanding and seemingly secure realm, but with deep and growing social inequalities and injustice. This picture is derived from two sources: the account of the reign of Jeroboam son of Joash in 2 Kgs 14.23-29, and the book of Amos itself. But whatever the historical value of the information in 2 Kgs 14.25, 28, it has a limited scope. It simply tells us that Jeroboam was successful in taking back territory that had been lost to the Aramaeans in the previous century. It does not tell us anything about the economic condition of Israel. Neither, for that matter, does the book of Amos. It does appear to witness to exploitation of the poor by a wealthy ruling class; but this could be because the latter were themselves under financial pressure, rather than living in the lap of luxury—and on that point commentators tend to accept the viewpoint of the text and elaborate on it, rather than adopting a critical stance (see Clines 1995). Moreover, there is no way of being certain that any particular assertion in the book does refer to the mid-eighth century rather than a later time (in this respect Houston 2004: 142-45 is too optimistic).

Archaeological evidence offers a rather different picture. Already in 1982 Jan Kees de Geus could write that 'A study of the material culture of Israel in the Iron Age reveals a detectable impoverishment… in the Iron IIC period. The turning point falls at the beginning of the eighth century, during Jeroboam II's reign in Israel' (de Geus 1982: 54, my translation). De Geus points to the Assyrian tribute demands as an explanation (55), but these only began in the second half of the century. It could be that Jeroboam's military adventures took up the available resources at the expense of building work. But whatever the explanation, it is generally financial stringency rather than prosperity that induces ruling classes to increase their pressure on the poor (cf. Houston 2004: 146). We shall take up the social question below.

Miller and Hayes, in their history of Israel and Judah, fix the 'decline' of Israel to the 'final years' of Jeroboam (2006: 354) rather than to his entire reign, maintaining that all the surrounding states, except Judah, were hostile, and that with the temporary decline of Assyrian power, on which Israel had relied, it was 'shut off from the larger world of trade and commerce'. In addition, they maintain, the kingdom was divided between rival claimants to the throne, following Cook 1964. Pekah is stated in 2 Kgs 15.27 to have had a reign of 20 years, which seems impossible to fit into the available space of time. The solution according to Cook is that Pekah dated his own reign not from his seizure of the throne in Samaria (2 Kgs 15.25), but from the beginning of his reign as a rival king in Gilead (east of the Jordan), where his supporters came from. Hayes uses this split in the kingdom as an important key in the interpretation of the text of Amos (Hayes 1988: 27). Pekah was a close associate of Rezin king of Damascus (2 Kgs 15.37; 16.5; Isa. 7.1-9), and this is the enemy that Amos had in mind, according to Hayes.

The Date of the Earthquake
The dating of Amos's prophetic activity 'two years before the earthquake' (1.1) shows that contemporaries were impressed by this aspect of his prophecy when the country was struck by a very violent earthquake. This was probably the most severe earthquake ever to strike the Levant in historical times. Its memory was still vivid when Zechariah 14 was written, perhaps as much as 400 years later. Isaiah 2.12-17, 5.25, and 9.9 may be contemporary allusions. Its archaeological traces, geological character, and date are all discussed by Austin, Franz and Frost 2000. It is evidenced by collapsed or leaning buildings at levels that have been carbon-14 dated to periods all bracketing the middle of the eighth century. Their precise date of 750 BCE (Austin *et al.* 2000: 664) is based on Josephus, *Ant.* 9.225, who

dates it to the first year of Jotham's regency, associating it with Uzziah's sacrilege related in 2 Chron. 26.16-21; and this is 750 according to Thiele's dating of the Hebrew kings (Thiele 1983; Miller and Hayes give 759). But it should be obvious that Josephus's dating owes more to theology than history. All that can be said is that there was a severe earthquake some time in the middle of the century, but it does not help to date Amos more precisely, though it does confirm that he was active in mid-century.

Refugees from Israel in Judah

The pivotal event for the creation of the book of Amos was probably the fall of Samaria to the Assyrians in 722, and the end of the kingdom, even if the earthquake was also significant. The present book has a Judaean viewpoint (see Chapter 7). Either the tradition of Amos's words was maintained in Judah from the beginning, or at some point it was taken from Israel to Judah. Fleming (2012) has a general and extensive discussion of how traditions from the kingdom of Israel have come to form part of the Jewish Bible. More specifically, it has been widely held that large numbers of refugees fled from the Assyrians over the border to Jerusalem, bringing with them some of the literary materials, both written and oral, that eventually found their way into the Hebrew Bible. The view that the number of refugees was large has recently been questioned (Na'aman 2014). But a *large* number of refugees is not required to carry a cultural tradition. The most obvious reason for fleeing would be to avoid deportation, and this was the fate mainly of the elite. And the scribal groups and other bearers of tradition would be found again mainly in the elite. Thus even small groups of Israelite migrants could have had a significant influence on the religious and literary inheritance of Judah.

2. *The Religious Context*

Monotheism or Polytheism?

As we have seen (above, p. 43), the basic theology of the book of Amos is, in Gowan's phrase, a 'practical monotheism'. We have also seen that the book of Amos makes almost no reference to the issue that dominates the book of Hosea, that is, the worship of gods other than Yhwh. H.M. Barstad's attempt to prove the contrary has been generally rejected (above, p. 42). The two verses that do appear to make such reference, 5.26 and 8.14, have each been very variously interpreted. But there is widespread agreement that the deities mentioned in 5.26 are Assyrian star gods. It is quite possible that Assyrian gods were worshipped after the Assyrian conquest, or even after heavy Assyrian political influence had begun to be felt, around 740. But this does not give any hint of the native polytheism that Hosea appears to lament.

We may no doubt agree with Barton that 'polytheism was the normal religion of Israel in practice' (Barton 2012: 56), given the strength of the evidence for it. Zevit offers a synthesis of the evidence from inscriptions, place names and personal names (Zevit 2001: 648-52). But this does very little to provide context for the book of Amos, which assumes not only that Yhwh is the god *of* Israel, but that no other god is of importance *in* Israel. The cultic practices that are satirized or dismissed are all addressed to Yhwh, and the sanctuaries attacked in 4.5 are sanctuaries of Yhwh: most of the attacks would lose their point if they were not.

The simple explanation is that the state god and the god of the people of Israel as a whole was Yhwh. That is, Yhwh was revered as the protector of Israel's state and people, the source of blessing, help and victory for them, and the ultimate source of authority in the kingdom. The oracles against the nations suggest that their hearers or readers take for granted that Yhwh has power over the whole world (Barton 2012: 58). This is generally true for the principal god of ancient peoples: thus the Babylonians, while worshipping many gods, express in their creation myth *Enuma elish* the claim of Marduk, the city god of Babylon, to be king of the gods, creator of the world, and supreme over the earth.

The significance of this is that the denunciations of the book are made against the state and people, and individual oracles primarily against upper-class groups who would be identified with the state. Those attacked may have honoured other gods in their private religious practices, but it is not these that are in the book's sights. The attacks on cultic practices refer exclusively to the pilgrimage festivals at the principal sanctuaries, which would have been frequented largely by the elites (see above, pp. 27-28), seeking blessing and help for the kingdom, fertility and prosperity for its agriculture, victory for its armies, and confirmation for its authority structure. The injustice and corruption attacked by the book concerns especially those attending the festivals of Yhwh; private and local cults are not so significant.

The Question of Bethel

The chief temple of the kingdom of Israel at Bethel, close to the border with Judah, figures prominently in the book of Amos, invariably in a bad light. At one point (4.5) two other pilgrimage sites, Gilgal and Beersheba, are associated with it, but otherwise Bethel stands alone. Many scholars have argued that a significant factor in the development of the book of Amos was rivalry between Jerusalem and Bethel as pilgrimage sanctuaries, either in the reign of Josiah of Judah (640–610 or 609) (Wolff 1977: 111-12, Coote 1981: 48-53) or later, even in the early Persian period according to a few scholars (Davies 2009). (See below, p. 71.) So how long did Bethel function as a temple and pilgrimage site after it ceased to be the sanctuary of the destroyed kingdom? Another question raised by some is whether Bethel could have been the site at which some Israelite literature, including the book of Amos, was first collected and transmitted to Judah.

It is not controversial that Bethel continued as a sanctuary, and therefore presumably as a pilgrimage site, until at least the late seventh century. Its continuance after the Assyrian annexation is implied in 2 Kgs 17.28; admittedly the story is historically unreliable, but that Bethel continued as a temple of Yhwh is likely to be one of the facts on which it is based. This is also assumed in 2 Kgs 23.15, which relates Josiah's doings there. It has usually been assumed, taking as historical the whole story in 2 Kgs 23.15-18, that at that point the sanctuary was defiled, if not destroyed, and fell into disuse.

Some writers, however (e.g. Blenkinsopp 2003; Knauf 2006), have argued, from indirect evidence, that in fact the temple did continue in use, and even became the chief sanctuary of Judah after the destruction of the Jerusalem temple and the end of the kingdom of Judah in 587. Once Jerusalem had been restored (in 515 according to Ezra 6.14-15), there would have been rivalry between them until Jerusalem decisively prevailed. More recently, however, considerable doubt has been thrown on this in any case largely speculative account (Finkelstein and Singer-Avitz 2009). In the later sixth century it was 'at best, a very small site' (Faust 2012b: 219). The conclusion should be that rivalry between the sanctuaries, or, better, a Judaean attempt to suppress pilgrimage to Bethel in favour of Jerusalem, is only likely in the late seventh century or the early sixth.

Relying on the same evidence, Fleming reaches the following conclusion concerning the function of Bethel as a site where Israelite traditions could have been gathered. 'The logical period for Bethel's influence on the formation and transmission of Israelite biblical tradition would be the eighth and early seventh centuries… This period matches perfectly the settings and reception of Hosea and Amos's (Fleming 2012: 320). While this is a satisfactory explanation for the emergence of the book of Hosea, for Amos we must take into account the fact that the book makes Amos himself a Judaean, presumably on the basis of some oral tradition or direct eyewitness, since the material of the book, after 1.1, does not say so, though 7.13 may hint at it. It is therefore equally or more likely that the material began to be shaped in Judah from the start.

3. *The Social Context*

Above (pp. 33-35), we sketched a picture of the social context implied by the condemnations in the book of Amos. But this is not social analysis. The victims of injustice are described as poor, but with barely any other detail. Their oppressors are not identified at all, though it is clear that they are (at least relatively) wealthy and that their base is primarily Samaria. What is the social structure that facilitates the oppression denounced here? What roles in the structure are played by the oppressors and the oppressed? Is the text describing an entire corrupt society or exceptional abuses? In answering these questions, commentators too often have simply taken their cue from the text itself, and filled in the details imaginatively. We need external evidence and some social theory.

The questions have been tackled by several writers, whether in relation to Amos alone (Lang 1983; Fleischer 1989: 346-423), to the prophetic literature, or parts of it (Dearman 1988; Chaney 1993; Houston 2004), or to the whole Hebrew Bible (Kippenberg 1977; Chaney 1986; Kessler 2008: 103-17; Gottwald 1993; Simkins 1999; Domeris 2007; Guillaume 2012; Boer 2015). Often, in the absence of adequate external evidence, they have fitted what we know into the framework of a model drawn from sociological literature or from known social processes in other places and times. I have compared various models, taking into account some of the archaeological evidence, mainly as gathered by Avraham Faust (Houston 2008: 18-51). Faust has since published a large and important synthesis in English on the societies of Israel and Judah as revealed by archaeology (Faust 2012b; see also Holladay 1995). Boer 2015 appeared too late for me to use.

The subject may be broken down into the following questions, and we will take them one by one. There is no space here for a full investigation, but I shall briefly indicate how the question has been, or might be, answered. First, what was the overall socio-political character of the society of Israel and Judah during the making of the book of Amos? Secondly, what positions were held, or functions exercised, within this social structure, by people of different social classes? Thirdly, can the activities denounced in the text be explained in social terms, and what relationships or transactions did they arise out of? We shall pay most attention here to the earliest period, the time when Amos is said to have been active, and immediately afterwards before the end of the eighth century, as in most cases redaction critics have not seen the oracles of judgment against oppression as redactional (see the next chapter). The main exception is 8.4-6, which is seen by a number of critics (e.g. Jeremias 1998: 145) to derive from Judah in the late pre-exilic period. Faust's evidence is mainly from the eighth century in Israel, and from the eighth and seventh in Judah.

The Society of Ancient Israel and Judah

Monarchic Israel and Judah are widely identified as 'agrarian societies' in Gerhard Lenski's sense (Lenski 1966: 189-296; accepting this, e.g. Faust 2012b: 270). Such societies contain two main classes, besides smaller classes of service workers: a large class of peasants cultivating the soil and a small governing class, typically no more than 5% of the population, who appropriate for themselves something like half of the country's wealth through taxes, tithes, rents and forced labour, and leave the peasants with a bare subsistence. It should be mentioned, however, that much of the portion appropriated by way of taxes goes not on the personal enrichment of the elite but to support the military establishment.

Guillaume (2012: 152) observes that the category of 'agrarian society' is so broad as to be almost valueless without further definition. Lenski himself admits that his description may need qualification for smaller states or ones less powerful in their own territory, so called 'simpler' societies: in these the degree of exploitation of the peasantry may be less developed. Faust suggests that Judah was a 'simple agrarian society', and Israel an 'advanced' one (2012b: 270), owing to its greater degree of urbanization and the development, in the cities, of more than two social classes. A variant idea refers to the social system of Israel (and Judah) as a 'tributary mode of production' (Gottwald 1993; Chaney 1986, 1993; see my discussion, Houston 2008: 35-43).

I would question whether Israel had reached the fully developed stage of an exploitative agrarian society by the time of the Assyrian conquest. Excavated Israelite villages of Iron II (the monarchic period) in the hill country do not show the signs of exploitation demonstrated by the villages of the valleys in the north of the country. Faust argues that these are likely to represent enclaves of conquered non-Israelite people, with whole villages owned by Israelite landowners or by the crown (Faust 2012b: 248-54, following Chaney 1986: 60-69). The hill-country villages, on the other hand, seem to have been occupied by an independent peasantry that was able to retain some surpluses (Holladay 1995: 391-93; Domeris 2007: 127-29), and was judged capable, around 740, of sustaining a special tax to pay for the Assyrian tribute demand (2 Kgs 15.19-20; see Houston 2004: 139-40). There was a tradition of tribal resistance to state domination reflected in such texts as 1 Sam. 8.11-18 and 1 Kings 12, and I have suggested that the state may have paid respect to this tradition (Houston 2008: 38-39), while ruthlessly exploiting non-Israelites. Another possible source of income for the state was the transit trade in luxuries (Holladay 1995: 382-86).

Fleischer (1989: 370-84) argues that population increase and the consequent division of inherited land into smaller and smaller plots contributed to the growing pauperization of the peasantry. Against this one may set, besides the lack of evidence of pauperization in the material remains, Bendor's opinion that inheritances were restricted to the two eldest sons and younger sons had limited rights, while weaker elements such as the widows of deceased brothers were often forced out (Bendor 1996: 173-94). Alternatively, Guillaume argues that there was no shortage of land (Guillaume 2012: 2 and passim).

This does not mean, however, that the farming population was immune to exploitation. Many farmers lived in the (so-called) cities, which were original villages taken over by the state and fortified as centres of power. Unlike the villages, these were marked by a sharp division between social classes, and kinship networks were likely to have been weaker (Faust 2012b: 110-17). It is the cities that define Israel as a state (Faust 2012b: 190-96). They were controlled by a royal official who probably combined the roles of governor, military commander and judge. It was the building of cities that enabled the kingdom to control its territory, yet at the same time it gave rise to a class of local power-holders. Officials would have been given land to support themselves, in place of a salary, and in time such 'prebends', as they are known, could easily have become hereditary.

At the apex of the social pyramid stood the king. He certainly bene-fited more than anyone from the upward flow of wealth. Yet there was a social expectation that he should defend the poor from exploitation (Ps. 72.2, 12-14; Jer. 22.3, 15-16: these are Judaean texts, but the ideology was widespread in the ancient Near East), and it was in his interest to repress the accumulation of power by other members of the elite (Houston 2008: 147). Thus the monarchy may have operated to some extent as a moderating or balancing influence within society.

A less favoured competitor for the description of the society of ancient Israel and Judah is as an 'ancient class society', like those of ancient Greece and Rome (Kippenberg 1977; Kessler 2008: 103-17; discussion Houston 2008: 31-35), dominated by aristocrats who attempted to control the peas-ants' land and appropriate their surplus, but were opposed by the peasants, leading to a compromise which protected them from losing their land or being enslaved. But these societies were not monarchies, and though there are protective measures in the Torah similar to those adopted in Greece, there is not much evidence that they were ever effective. My conclusion is that if there was a development towards 'ancient class society', it was abor-tive (Houston 2008: 34).

In summary, we may define eighth-century Israel as a tribal kingdom, that is, a monarchy built on the support of an ethnic group, but sharply divided between its ruling class and the rest, a stratification seen most easily in the cities, where the ruling class lived.

The Social Roles of Poor People and Others

It has been almost universally assumed that the poor in Israel and Judah were the peasants, and that their oppressors were city-dwellers, whether land-lords exacting rents (argued in detail by Lang 1983), or officials demanding taxes and labour service, and probably exceeding their remit for personal gain, and judges making corrupt judgments in their favour. It is argued that in the 'tributary mode of production' there was no distinction between tax and rent, since the whole land was held to belong to the crown. The assump-tion that the poor were peasants is not unreasonable, since the main source of wealth was the cultivation of the soil, hence the enrichment of unproductive classes must have been directly or indirectly at their expense (Domeris 2007).

But there are a number of qualifications that must be made to this generalization. Most of the rural population lived in the kinship-based villages already mentioned, where the co-operative ethos would usually have ensured that any burden was fairly distributed. In Israel, Israelite villages were probably not subject to forced labour (Houston 2008: 38-39), and, as I argue below, may well not have been subject to state taxes (as distinct from tithes) until the advent of the Assyrians. On the other hand, the inhabitants of non-Israelite villages, cultivating their land perhaps as sharecroppers, may well have been left with a bare minimum; and farmers living in the socially divided cities, without the protection of the kinship network, were much more exposed to exploitation of various kinds. In the cities there were many other people who would have counted as poor, and might also be exploited: artisans and small traders, those who could only scratch a living as day labourers, and others who were altogether without a livelihood. I have argued, following Faust, that most of the references to oppression in the prophets could refer to what they could see before their eyes in the capital cities (Houston 2010a; see esp. 108-109).

Those in a position to exploit the poor would have been equally varied: officials responsible for taxation or for the crown estates, judges in the royal courts (clearly in view in several places in Isaiah), owners of land in the neighbourhood of the capital, or indeed in any part of the country, who lived in the capital for its advantages in access to power and convenience. Amos mentions Samaria as the seat of the oppressors several times: 3.9; 3.12; 4.1; 6.1. One group frequently mentioned in the literature is merchants (see especially Guillaume 2012). In all probability there was no class of merchants in eighth-century Israel (cf. Polanyi 1957: 259, who asserts this of 'archaic society in general'). There would have been local traders in the cities, who were not members of the elite; on the other hand long-distance trade was probably mainly in the hands of foreigners or of officials acting on behalf of the crown (Polanyi 1957: 259-62). Those whom we find selling corn in Amos 8.4-6 may be officials: it has been suggested that the sale of grain in the cities, or at least in the capitals, could have been a crown monopoly, though there is no definite evidence to that effect (Fleischer 1989: 192-93; Houston 2008: 64).

Another approach is to suggest that not all oppression was the work of elites. Bendor (1996: 231-32) argues that neither the kinship network of the village (the *mišpāḥâ*) nor the extended family (*bêt 'āb*) was a society of equals; the *bêt 'āb* in particular was under the absolute authority of its head, and some members were more vulnerable than others, such as younger brothers or the widow and children of a deceased brother. The head might act oppressively, for example in deciding who to hand over to a cred-itor as security for a debt. This is how Bendor explains Amos 2.6: 'because they sell the one who has rights [i.e. in the family inheritance] for silver...' (1996: 246-48). The hypothesis is plausible in itself, but it is difficult to apply it to much else in Amos, where it is usually clear that the culprits are to be found in Samaria or elsewhere among the ruling class.

The Mechanisms of Oppression
A whole range of relationships or transactions has been proposed as pos-sible sites for the various oppressions that are vaguely denounced in the prophets, and many of them are obvious or at least plausible. Some of them are public, e.g. taxation and the corvée (forced labour), or cases in court, others are private, e.g. the relationships of landlord and tenant, creditor and debtor, seller and buyer (in Amos 8.4-6).

The one overarching private relationship that is the key to much that goes on in societies outside modern northern Europe and North America is *patronage* (see Simkins 1999; Domeris 2007: 87-92; Houston 2008: 44-48; all dependent on Eisenstadt and Roniger 1984, among others). In this rela-tionship the *client* seeks help from a more powerful citizen, the *patron*, for example to supply provisions in a time of dearth, or to protect him (the par-ties are nearly always male) against the depredations of a corrupt tax collec-tor. In return the client gives the patron his loyalty and support in political conflicts, together with gifts from time to time, which may be accumulated to provide a buffer against hard times for the patron's many clients (Dom-eris 2007: 88). This is the typical way in which the Hebrew Bible conceives of the relationship between unequal parties: see for example the idealis-tic picture in Job 29.7-25 (Houston 2008: 127-29; criticized in Guillaume 2012: 159-60). Job meets the need of all who apply to him, and in return he achieves unparalleled honour in his own community. More realistically, Lev. 25.35-40 envisages someone in difficulties, a fellow-member of the people of Israel, being supported by a patron, and offering labour in return. (NRSV 'Any of your kin' [v. 35] is a bit misleading.) Domeris appears to assume that most peasant farmers in Israel (and Judah) would owe duties to a patron, whether in their own village or a nearby city. But it is likely that strong kinship networks still dominated the villages (cf. Guillaume 2012: 155-56), and this would perform functions similar to those of a patron, only the situation would be more symmetrical: that is, you would receive help from kin (or neighbour) in hard times, and would be expected to offer help, not necessarily to the same person, when you were better placed. Things would probably be different for peasants in the cities, and here patronage may have loomed larger.

Where the relationship works as it should, both parties benefit; but because the patron is in a position of power over the client, he can easily abuse it to gain unfair advantage. Domeris speaks of the reciprocity inherent in the patron-client relationship as breaking down in this situation and becoming 'negative reciprocity', where 'violence becomes a substitute for obligation'; and he asserts that 'the tone and character of Prophetic texts indicates that sometime [*sic*] in the Iron Age... positive reciprocity collapsed in Israel and Judah'—i.e. not as an abuse on the part of some, but universally (Domeris 2007: 90). This may be true, but it is difficult to prove, owing to the tendency of prophetic texts to hyperbole, or the need of editors to provide justification for the downfall of the kingdoms (Barton 1990).

There is more than one way in which patronage may be abused. One of the most well known is through credit. Poor people often need loans when they are in financial difficulty, and this is less humiliating than pure charity: but the patron may use this as an opportunity to obtain labour service by making the client give up a son or daughter in debt bondage either as security for the loan or to work off an unpaid debt (2 Kgs 4.1; Neh. 5.5); or the debtor himself could give his labour service (Lev. 25.39-40). Thus the patron-client relationship may also involve the relationship of master and slave: the Leviticus text just quoted is an attempt to soften the harshness of this. Often a young girl in debt-bondage would be subject to sexual abuse (see Exod. 21.7-11). This may be the background of Amos 2.7b. Guillaume, however, argues that parents would benefit from having their children taken off their hands (2012: 166-68). But given that they were old enough to work, they would be as valuable to their parents as to any creditor.

Guillaume insists that it is normal for farmers to be in debt, that credit is essential to agriculture, and that it sets up a relationship between the farmer and the merchant (whom he takes to be the creditor) that is to the benefit of both; so a farmer can be permanently in debt without its affecting his independence, provided that he can regularly repay some of what he owes (Guillaume 2012: 111-49). This argument depends on evidence from economies more complex than that of monarchic Israel, where agriculture would have been primarily for subsistence. Guillaume also dismisses the idea that anyone would lend money to a poor person who could not repay (168): but since he himself argues that one object of lending was to obtain labour service, this does not seem to follow.

Another impact of debt on peasants is to lose their land, either all or some of it, whether by forfeiting security or by sale; but again there is no evidence that this was generally happening in Israel at the time of Amos.

The landlord-tenant relationship has been asserted to be central to the book of Amos (see especially Lang 1982; also Domeris 2007: 103-104; Anderson and Freedman 1989: 500). However, as I have argued (Houston 2008: 29), it is hard to believe that such an institution as leasehold tenure existed at all in Israel or Judah before the Hellenistic period, since the vocabulary of biblical Hebrew does not include any words that certainly relate to it. Some will have worked the land under the authority of a landowner, perhaps as debt-slaves, and there were crown estates, worked perhaps by slaves, perhaps by conscript labour; but, as we have seen, Israelites in the highland villages remained independent up to the fall of the kingdom.

Public relationships include taxation, forced labour for the state (the corvée), corruption in the courts, and the corruption and violent behaviour of public officials.

We know very little about taxation in monarchic Israel and Judah, despite detailed accounts of how it purportedly worked (e.g. Chaney 1993), which are frankly pure speculation. I would suggest a few basic theses, however, which may cast a rather different light on the matter. Normally in ancient ethnic states, nationals were not taxed. 'Generally speaking, tribute was levied only on conquered populations' (Graeber 2011: 63; see Mt. 17.25-26). To be sure, Graeber admits exceptions, including pharaonic Egypt (2011: 400 n. 51). But in monarchic Israel, as noted above, there are clear signs of conquered populations being treated differently, and it is likely that Israelites expected to be free of taxes. Is it then possible that the reason why Menahem's 50-shekel poll tax alone is mentioned in Kings (2 Kgs 15.20) is that it was the only tax that Israelites had *ever* been asked to pay since the days of Jeroboam I (though it is likely that there were more to come)? Amos 5.11 is generally thought to refer to taxes, but there are other possibilities (see below). I have already suggested that Israelites were not subject to the corvée, but non-Israelites certainly were (see Judg. 1.28, 30, 32, 33; Josh. 9.21; 1 Kgs 9.20-21; Houston 2008: 39). Even though most of these texts are set in pre-monarchic times, they can only have been a reality under the kings: it takes a state to enforce such violence.

We may then tentatively rule out imposts of tax or labour, imposed by proper authority, as being significant modes of exploitation of Israelites in monarchic Israel before the Assyrian advance. But we cannot rule out unauthorized exactions by corrupt officials, still less distortions of the judicial process: bribes, biased or corrupt judges, and false witness. Such things are extremely common in less developed countries today (and not unknown in more developed ones!), and in view of the frequency of the warnings against such things in the Torah, including one of the Ten Commandments, as well as attacks in the prophets, we can be sure that they were common features of life. Certain texts of Amos undoubtedly refer to them (5.10, 12), and others may do so; most commentators regard 2.6b as referring to sale into slavery (perhaps with a bribe: Paul 1991: 77-79), but Domeris has revived the older interpretation with regard to the bribery of judges (Domeris 2007: 112; Hammershaimb 1970: 46; cf. Cripps 1955: 140). The corn-sellers in 8.4-6 were probably required to sell at a fixed price, which explains why they falsified the price for underhand gain.

Drawing again from the experience of less developed countries today, we may easily suppose that the powerful are able to use pressure or even open violence to get their way, precisely because they are powerful and hence immune to prosecution. Hence the language of violence that Amos uses, in 2.7a; 3.10; 5.7, 12 may well be meant literally in every case, as also certainly the language of fraud in 8.5-6.

To sum up, the social context of the text of Amos is that of a state with a relatively simple but sharply stratified class structure, in which urbanization and the development of state institutions, with the enrichment of state officials, gave opportunity to the powerful to gain further power and wealth through the abuse of patronage, corrupt practices, and simple violence, exercised primarily against those whose poverty and loss of a strong kinship network, again through urbanization, made them less able to resist exploitation. It is impossible to say how widespread such abuses were. One should note the particularity of the accusations, and take into account the tendency to rhetorical exaggeration in prophecy, along with the function of theodicy given to it by its editors, before rushing as commentators tend to do to write off Israelite society as totally corrupt and exploitative.

Further Reading

Unless you have a thorough knowledge of ancient Israelite and Judaean history already, a good up-to-date history book is essential. Miller and Hayes 2006 is the standard (the ever-popular Bright is long past its sell-by date), but it should be supplemented by Grabbe 2007, which discusses what we can really know, and how.

For the archaeology, Mazar 1990: 403-550 is still a good general account, but Faust 2012b is the only book (but see Holladay 1995) primarily devoted to attempting to deduce what can be known of the *societies* of Israel and Judah from the archaeological remains, though it must be admitted that Faust perhaps draws over-confident conclusions from evidence that is always difficult to evaluate.

On the social issues, the books offering a broad overview include Houston 2008: 18-51, Domeris 2007, Guillaume 2012 and Boer 2015. I may not be expected to give an unbiased opinion of my own work, but others might say that in this revised edition (as also here) I give too much weight to Faust's conclusions, as distinct from his evidence. Guillaume is worth reading for a view sharply critical of most readings of the situation by biblical scholars. He gives a knowledgeable account of the sociology and economics of farming in the Near East, but his exegesis of relevant biblical texts is idiosyncratic and not necessarily well-founded. Unlike Guillaume, Domeris and perhaps I are insufficiently critical of prophetic hyperbole. For the 'tributary mode of production', see Gottwald 1993; for 'rent capitalism' Lang 1985; for patronage Simkins 1999. Those who read German may benefit from Fleischer's detailed discussion and distinctive approach (Fleischer 1989: 346-423).

Chapter 7

THE MAKING OF THE BOOK OF AMOS

Amos the Man

Most commentaries on Amos begin by saying something about Amos the man and his times, generally taken to be the mid-eighth century BCE. We have not done that in this book, but rather begun with a study of the *text* of Amos, for two reasons: firstly because the text is what we have, and it is best to move from what we know to what is less certainly known; and secondly because it is increasingly questioned whether we in fact know anything about the prophet Amos, or even, occasionally, whether he existed at all.

All the same, it is still assumed in most commentaries and other scholarly works that we can use the information in 1.1 and 7.10-17 to construct a picture of Amos. According to this, Amos was active round about 760 BCE (the basis of this dating is rather insecure, but see e.g. Mays 1969: 20), and came from Tekoa in Judah. It is not altogether clear what his profession was. Was he a humble shepherd, as 7.14 suggests, or rather a master 'sheep breeder' (1.1: the same word is used in 2 Kgs 3.4 of the king of Moab). He understood himself to have been called by Yhwh to prophesy to the kingdom of Israel (7.15). He appeared at Samaria and at Bethel, and perhaps at other places such as Gilgal, and delivered (most of) the prophecies of judgment that are found in the book of Amos. He came to the attention of the authorities, and was instructed by Amaziah, the priest in charge of the sanctuary of Bethel, to return home to Judah. Amaziah appears to imply that Amos earned his living as a prophet (compare e.g. Mic. 3.5), and this Amos denies. He prophesied because Yhwh had called him to do so, and not because it was his profession.

As this is the entire stock of information provided by the book, accounts diverge at this point. Did he return to Judah or did he defy Amaziah and meet a martyr's death, as ancient tradition relates (see Jeremias 1998: 2)? Did he have a group of disciples who wrote down his words and to whom he related his visions? How did his words become a book? None of these questions can be definitely answered from the available evidence.

And while the account, so far as it goes, is plausible enough, it falls far short of being secure history. The story in 7.10-17 has often been regarded as a much later composition, and effectively fictional (Ackroyd 1977; Radine 2010: 183-97). Most of the information in 1.1 can be seen as having been derived from the contents of the book, especially from 7.10-17, plus the book of Kings, which makes Jeroboam II partially contemporary with Uzziah (=Azariah: 2 Kgs 14.23; 15.1-2). The only items that could not have been derived from the contents of the book by an editor are Amos's origin from Tekoa, and that he prophesied 'two years before the earthquake'.

Although it has been argued that much of the book's material is typical of 'tribal wisdom' (Wolff 1973), a fundamental difficulty in accepting that the book that we have originates from the work of a simple countryman is its sophisticated artistic style and structure, which we have already explored. This book, whatever may lie behind it, is a product of scribal culture. To place the book of Amos in history is to account for the process by which some oral prophecies became a literary work—if indeed there were any prophecies to start with. How do we account for the book as it stands? What is its relation to the work of the prophet Amos?

A Spectrum of Views

The basic question, how much of the book goes back to Amos, has been answered in many different ways, which may be classified in three groups:

(a) Many scholars believe the whole book, or virtually the whole book, represents directly or indirectly the work of Amos: e.g. Rudolph, Andersen and Freedman, Paul, Hayes.

(b) On the other extreme, some treat the book as a purely literary work, perhaps based on or including some fragments going back to a prophet of the eighth century; but these would be hypothetical and impossible to identify with any security: e.g. Coggins (2000), Davies (2009), also Linville (2000). Radine (2010) and Kratz (2011) straddle this group and the next: Amos is a literary work with no connection (Radine) or only a little (Kratz) with real prophecy, but the book was developed in stages through redaction.

(c) The majority of critical scholars trace a process of redaction, with earlier and later layers, and most believe that the earliest layer of the book consists of, or is closely related to, Amos's own words; hence this group claims to be able to explain the *process* by which oral prophecies became a literary work. Representative of this approach are Wolff 1977; Coote 1981; Jeremias 1998; Hadjiev 2009; Barton 2012.

The views on offer depend heavily on prior assumptions. The authors in group (a) assume that any particular text will come from Amos unless there is good reason to suppose otherwise. Those in group (b) require good reason to suppose that any text *does* come from Amos. So in examining these views, we shall have to look at the arguments *against* them, the 'good reasons' that might, but do not, persuade their proponents otherwise. However good the reason, it is always possible to find counter-reasons. Hence an author's view will tend to be determined by his or her general approach to the biblical text, conservative, liberal or sceptical. Nevertheless, there are points where an uncommitted reader will tend to be persuaded in a particular direction.

'All comes from Amos'

The writers who take this view do not necessarily agree on the way in which Amos's prophecies became a book, or on its purpose. Paul has a sense of the course of Amos's ministry which is not reflected in the arrangement of the book, and he appears to imply, without actually saying so, that it was Amos himself who arranged it in literary form (Paul 1991: 4).

Anderson and Freedman, on the other hand, have a clear answer to both questions: the book is 'a memorial for Amos and a monument for posterity', which 'comes from Amos himself, representing a comprehensive synthesis and testament prepared either by him or by an immediate disciple' (Anderson and Freedman 1989: 10-11). But it is hard to see why Amos should have wanted to set up 'a monument for posterity'. The fulfilment of his message would be his monument! (cf. Coote 1981: 42-43).

Hayes (1988: 39) dismisses the notion of a circle of disciples and thinks it most likely that either Amos himself or someone in Amos's audience wrote down his speeches, which he believes were delivered over as little as a single day. But how some scrappy notes became the book that we have, or why they were preserved, is not explained; and if Amos was an author, he was not the man he claims to be in 7.14!

Criteria of Redaction

There are many reasons to believe that, contrary to these writers, the book of Amos includes materials coming from a later time than his. The criteria that are regularly used to detect the presence of redactional material are various. Hadjiev (2009: 25-40) has a careful discussion of both their advantages and their pitfalls. Barton's overview (2012: 41-51) shows very clearly how they apply to some prominent passages. Some of the more important are these; I have given only a few examples of how they may be applied, but those include several where more than one of them apply.

1. When a passage is clearly not of the same genre or style as those which surround it, that suggests it has been added (Hadjiev 2009: 26). The series of four visions, told in the first person, in chaps. 7-8, is broken by the third-person narrative in 7.10-17: indeed, it breaks even the closer connection between the second pair of visions. Other examples include 3.7, where a series of brief parallel poetic questions is broken by a long prose sentence making an assertion; and 6.2, where the series of descriptive addresses to those at ease (using participles in Hebrew: 6.1, 3, 4, 5, 6) is broken by two imperative sentences and a question. However, the fact that a text is in prose should not be taken on its own as a reason to regard it as redactional.

2. There are 'thematic tensions', as Hadjiev calls them (2009: 30-31), in the book, although overall it is remarkably coherent thematically. For example, the tentative suggestion of divine mercy in response to repentance and the establishment of justice in 5.14-15 is in tension with the confident assertion of restoration in 9.11-15 without any reference to repentance or justice (see Cripps 1955: 72-73). Even more significantly, we have already explored the tension between the oracles of judgment, addressed to particular powerful and wealthy people, and the disaster again and again prophesied for Israel as a nation. The fact that there is at least one verse resolving this tension (9.8) suggests that the final editors of the book felt it as a real one.

3. Some elements in the book appear to betray theological or linguistic features from times later than the eighth century. W.H. Schmidt devoted an influential article to 'Deuteronomistic' additions (Schmidt 1965), which he held can be identified both by their language and by their theology. The most obvious is the oracle against Judah (2.4-5). This accuses them of rejecting Yhwh's law, and not keeping his statutes, a definition of sin that is certainly typical of Deuteronomy. If, as Anderson and Freedman argue (1989: 294-306), this oracle comes from Amos, it is strange that Israel is not accused in the same way (Radine 2010: 17). Even more typical is 3.7 (cf. above): the idea of the prophets as 'Yhwh's servants' is often found in Kings.

4. There may be reference to later historical situations. There is hardly any question that 6.2 refers to victories by the Assyrians in the 730s, which is later than the time of Amos according to 1.1 and 7.9-10 (see all the commentaries; Paul [1990: 203] argues against). Another solution is to date Amos himself later (e.g. Coote 1981: 22; Strijdom 2011): but of course that involves seeing the connection with Jeroboam II created by 7.9-10 as a

move by a later editor (Ackroyd 1977; Coote 1981: 22; see also Radine 2010: 188-97). Most scholars would also see 9.11-15 as a response to the situation after the fall of Judah in 587 (but see Hayes 1988: 244).

In general, the supporters of the 'authenticity' of the entire book will always be able to say that such-and-such a feature *could* be considered credible in Amos's time and work. However, the balance of probability, considered without such a commitment, is on the side of viewing at least some passages as redactional. This is the conclusion of Barton's careful examination of the question.

Amos as a Scribal Creation

A increasingly widespread view is one at the opposite extreme from this: that the book is as a whole a literary creation, perhaps including some older prophetic oracles, but not owing its origin to a continuous process reaching back to an early collection of Amos's oracles, whether or not that process is seen as involving a great deal of editorial intervention, redactional addition, and updating.

From the Persian Period?

Coggins is largely agnostic about the origin of the book, though confident it was 'brought together in Jerusalem' (2000: 8), and dating it in the Second Temple period (76, later refined to the fifth century). 'Even if we assume that there is more ancient material now incorporated within the book, it is misleading to suppose that the particular thrust of such material can be recovered from an essentially later composition' (76). He also considers it uncertain whether Amos himself lived in the eighth century.

Davies views the production of the book of Amos as part of a larger project producing authoritative books in Persian period Jerusalem. He suggests that there may have been archives of prophetic sayings preserved and filed under the name of the prophet, similar to those found at Mari and in the Assyrian royal archives, which would have been drawn on by scribes in the Persian period creating 'prophetic' books for their own purposes (Davies 2000: 73-75). This would not mean there was any continuous collection of Amos's words before this.

Reasons to Believe that the Book of Amos was not first Composed in the Persian Period

These are well set out by Hadjiev (2009: 12-17). Among the more important are these:

1. 'The description of punishment is too general and does not seem
    to reflect the experience of later times' (p. 12). Neither Assyria nor
    Babylon is mentioned; threats of exile are mixed with ones of earth-
    quake; the challenges of life under foreign rule are not reflected. 'It
    is Israel's power, not Israel's weakness, that is usually the prob-
    lem' (p. 12).
2. The oracles against the nations fit much better into a situation
    before 732 BCE, when the Aramaean kingdom of Damascus was
    conquered and turned into an Assyrian province. They begin with
    Damascus and end with Israel, neither of which survived the eighth
    century in independence. 'The geopolitical viewpoint of the creator
    of the series is an eighth-century one' (Houston 2004: 142).
3. Hope for restoration occupies a very insignificant part of the book:
    the 'roses and lavender' are a small corner of a canvas filled for
    the most part with 'blood and iron'. This is untypical of post-exilic
    work in the Prophets.
4. There are features of the picture of Israel in the text that are typical
    of the monarchic period: 'the pride of Jacob', or the fact that Israel
    has an army (2.14-16; 5.3) and has some military success (6.13).

A Literary Creation from the Monarchic Period?

Radine and Kratz both posit a first edition of the book composed not in the
Persian period, but after the fall of Samaria (Kratz 2011: 339; Radine 2010:
54-72), and accounting theologically for that event. Like most other scholars they see a process of redaction in stages up to the Persian period. But
unlike the majority, and like Davies, they do not conceive of the first edition as a presentation of the words of Amos. The difference between them
is that Kratz claims to be able to isolate a few genuine 'words of Amos of
Tekoa' extended and reshaped into a new text with a purpose foreign to
Amos, while Radine sees no need to look for any genuine words of Amos at
all, since, according to him, the book is not a genuine book of prophecy, but
a 'literary-predictive text' under the guise of a collection of prophetic words
(110-29; see above, p. 8).

For Kratz, Amos was not a prophet of judgment (2011: 340). He recre-
ates Amos in the image of the ancient Near Eastern prophets that we know
about from the archives of Assyria and of the kingdom of Mari in Syria,
c. 1700 BCE, who did not predict final disaster for their societies (Kratz
2011: 316-17). The reconstructed Amos is not only not a prophet of judgment, he is not even a prophet of social justice. How and why has he been
made one? Kratz does not have an answer.

Radine also argues that the first edition of the book was composed in
the wake of the fall of Samaria, but as a 'literary-predictive text' it required

no pre-existing material. The book was composed in Judah, and addressed both Judaeans and Israelites who had fled to Jerusalem before or after the Assyrian conquest. 'It would have served a variety of purposes, including explaining the fall of the northern kingdom, strongly combating northern worship, and condemning the [lost] wealth of a people who... had moved into a formerly poorer country.' Parallels in Mesopotamian literature reveal two other purposes: 'to legitimate Judah as the new sole nation of Yahweh, and to avert the spread of Yahweh's wrath to the South' (140).

Most of Hadjiev's arguments against a Persian-period composition will not apply to Kratz and Radine, but two may do so. No. 1 above notes the vagueness and generality of the threats. This is a point not only against composition in the Persian period, but even in the late eighth century. Nothing of the specific events of 745–722 is reflected, only general references to defeat, invasion, death and deportation. Assyria is mentioned nowhere. The reference to the earthquake in 1.1, usually supposed to be the earliest element in the superscription, has nothing to do with the fall of Samaria, but it clearly reflects some of the threats in the book. More generally, as I have already pointed out (above, p. 9), the book does not resemble works which are usually recognized as 'prophecies' of past events, such as the book of Daniel.

Jeremias argues from the theme of the rejection of the prophet and his message of judgment, as in Amos 7.10-13. Kratz had seen this as simply a literary motif, bound up with the invention of judgment prophecy (2011: 42), but Jeremias points out there are texts that are evidence of a rejection of the prophetic word already at the oral stage, e.g. Hos. 9.7-9; Mic. 2.6-7 (he could have added Amos 3.8). Therefore judgment prophecy is not something only invented after the fall of Samaria. It is this rejection that leads to the initial writing down of prophetic words (Jeremias 2013: 104-105).

It is reasonable to conclude that prophets such as Amos did speak words of judgment upon their nation, that they experienced rejection as a consequence, and that however the books named after them have been expanded or developed, those words form their nucleus.

The Book of Amos is the Result of a Process of Redaction beginning with the Words of Amos

This third alternative is accepted by the great majority of critical scholars. Each scholar has a different solution in detail, but there is a wide measure of agreement. The texts identified by Barton as redactional (2012: 41-51) are the minimum accepted as such by most of those who accept the existence of redaction at all. They are 1.1, the superscription (accepted by everyone); 1.2, the so-called 'motto', from a 'Judaean edition of the book' (42); 1.9-12, the oracles against Tyre and Edom (historically problematic in Amos's time, and stylistically aligned with the Judah oracle); 2.4-5, the oracle against Judah (see above); 3.7 (see above); the 'hymns' or 'doxologies' at 4.13; 5.8-9; and 9.5-6 (strategically placed elements of the composition); possibly 5.25, 'Did you bring to me sacrifices...' (prose); 5.26-27 (prose, and Amos does not elsewhere attack idolatry); 7.10-17 (treated by Barton as giving genuine information *about* Amos); possibly 8.4-6 (another version of 2.6-8); 8.11-12 (untypical of Amos); probably 8.13-14; 9.8b, apparently added to 'mitigate the harshness' (48-49) of 9.8a; 9.9-10, as the idea of a distinction between sinners and righteous in the judgment is contrary to Amos's usual message (but see above, p. 27); 9.11-12, with its Jerusalem-centred and post-587 outlook (see above); and 9.13-15, typical of post-exilic prophecy.

Others would identify much more of the text as redactional. But in any case it is not sufficient to identify redactional texts if one wishes to understand the process. One must also be able to identify *compositions*: successive editions of the book of Amos created by its redactors, in each of which a set of additions and other adjustments plays a part in updating the book, and making it relevant to a new time and place (Hamborg 2012: 12-17). So each composition should be able to be dated, and, most importantly, its purpose in the political, religious and social situation of the day identified.

Again, there are points on which many or most scholars are in agreement. The present obvious threefold division of the book (see above, p. 19) is taken by many, not unreasonably, as a key to its history. Thus Wolff (1977: 107-8) regards chaps. 3-6 (minus later additions) as the original 'words of Amos... from Tekoa' referred to in 1.1, while the oracles against the nations and the visions form two series which closely correspond to each other and would have been fixed in writing at the same time, perhaps representing 'a more advanced stage of literary development' (107). But Wolff does think they go back to Amos. Jeremias's view (1998: 6) is similar. Hadjiev also bases his reconstruction of the history of the text on this division.

As for the date and place of composition, there is agreement among all but the most conservative scholars that the book that we now have reflects Judaean concerns and was probably completed in Judah in post-exilic times. The superscription's placing the king of Judah before Jeroboam, despite the fact that Amos is represented as preaching solely to Israel, and the fact that the book is framed by the opening words in 1.2 making Yhwh 'roar from Zion' and the assurance for 'the fallen/ing booth of David' in 9.11 show the point of view of the composition (Houston 2008: 59). That its completion was in post-exilic (Persian-period) times seems likely from the fact that it closes with salvation assurances typical of the period (Jeremias 1998: 162; Barton 2012: 50-51; Hamborg 2012: 92-98). Hadjiev, however, argues for the sixth century, the early Persian period at latest.

Going back to the beginning of the process, there is agreement among a wide range of scholars that the *first* written form of the book appeared not long after 722, with the object of dealing theologically with the fall of the kingdom of Israel and its consequences. Generally the place of composition is named as Judah, or more specifically Jerusalem. The composition would have shown that the disaster was just punishment for the nation's sins, willed by Yhwh, who proclaimed it beforehand by his prophet; and also functioned as a warning to Judah to avoid the same fate.

This dating is agreed by so conservative a scholar as Möller (2003: 119), and such radical ones as Kratz (2011: 339), and Radine (2010: 54-72; 140), with e.g. Jeremias (1998: 5) and Hamborg (2012: 111, 115) in between. As for the purpose or function of the composition, Hamborg's argument (2012: 111-12) is notable: that the invitations to 'seek Yhwh' in the central unit of the book, 5.1-17, alongside unconditional proclamations of judgment, which have been fulfilled for Israel, function as warning to those in Judah that 'they, too, must seek good and not evil...; they, too, must refrain from the very activities described in the reasons for judgment...falling on the northern kingdom' (112). Wolff, however (1977: 110), and Hadjiev (2009: 185-86) place the first written compositions before the fall of Samaria.

There are of course wide differences in scholars' assessment of the extent of that first composition and the frequency with which it underwent redaction. One of the respects in which scholars differ most widely is in the number of successive compositions that they identify, which varies from three (Coote 1981: perhaps only two, since he is agnostic about whether his 'stage A' existed in written form) to twelve (Rottzoll 1996). I now set out a selection of the theories that are available in English.

Theories of Redaction and Composition

Hans-Walter *Wolff* sets out six successive stages of composition in his influential commentary (1977: 106-13). The first two go back to Amos himself: respectively the core of the 'words of Amos' in chaps. 3–6; and the original five oracles against the nations in 1.3–2.16*, with the visions in 7.1–9.4*. He then sees disciples of Amos whom he calls 'the old school of Amos' as having combined these with material of their own, including the story of Amos and Amaziah in 7.10-17 (with 7.9), 5.14-15, and most of the material beyond the visions in chap. 8 and 9.7-10. Although these are closely related to Amos's message, the language is different. This work would have been completed in Judah, Amos's own country, before the fall of Samaria, around 735. There are then three groups of redactional additions. The first is what he calls 'the Bethel-exposition of the Josianic Age', i.e. the late seventh century. This makes it clear that worship at Bethel (desecrated by Josiah according to 2 Kgs 23.15) is no longer acceptable, including the references in 3.14 and 5.6; but Wolff also includes here the hymnic pieces in 4.13, 5.8-9 and 9.5-6, and the series 'you did not return to me' in 4.6-12 (Wolff 1977: 111, 217). The second is a Deuteronomistic redaction chiefly concerned to make Amos's message relevant to exilic Judah, including 2.4-5; 3.1b; 3.7; the reference to Zion in 6.1; 1.9-12; 2.10-12; and 5.25-26. The last is the post-exilic eschatology of salvation in 9.8b, 11-15.

Wolff's theories are important in setting the agenda for most subsequent redaction critics. Joachim *Jeremias* is indebted to him, but his proposals (summary in 1998: 5-9) are somewhat more radical. He identifies four different stages in the development of the book. The first edition of the book is made after, not before, the fall of Samaria. This edition corresponds to Wolff's first three layers taken together. Amos's sayings against limited groups 'are placed [in this edition] into a context that speaks throughout about the people of God as a whole' (7). And at the heart of this edition, Jeremias stresses (1998: 7), the ring-composition 5.1-17 demands justice as the condition for any possible hope of 'life' for the survivors of the catastrophe.

(The sections of the introduction in Jeremias 1998 are in a muddle. As a glance at the original shows (Jeremias 1995: XIX-XXI), the 'three respects' mentioned at the top of p. 7 refer to the next three paragraphs, which should be numbered 1, 2, 3. The '3.2' that follows is parallel in the original to a much earlier '3.1', which in the translation is replaced by an 'a.' (5) without any corresponding 'b.'!)

Jeremias retains a late pre-exilic redactional layer; but it includes most significantly the Amaziah episode, which along with 6.9-10; 8.3, 9-10 highlights the doom awaiting all Israel, and heightens the focus on Amos's prophetic authority. It also includes the accusation against the corn-dealers. He places the attack on Bethel and the hymnic pieces in the sixth century, unlike Wolff, along with the Deuteronomistic interventions, and the final edition is placed in post-exilic times rather than the sixth century. Hamborg, who follows Jeremias quite closely, provides a conspectus of these compositions (Hamborg 2012: 98), preceded by detailed argument on individual texts (45-98), and followed by discussion of the coherence and origins of the compositions (100-30).

Robert *Coote* (1981: 1-10) says that his theory is a simplification of Wolff's, as it only has three stages rather than six. But in fact his stage A, Amos's original oracles, is arrived at in a completely different way, by excluding everything which is not a poetic oracle of judgment against 'a specific class of persons' (16) for specific acts of oppression. It consists of: 2.6b-8*, 13-16; 3.9-11; 3.12; 4.1-3; 5.1-2 (excluding 'house of Israel'); 5.11a, 12b, 11b; 5.16-17; 5.18-20; 6.1-7 (with v. 2, dating Amos in the 730s); 6.8a, 11; 8.4-10; 9.1-4 (excluding 'I saw Yhwh standing on/by the altar, and he said') (Coote 1981: 11-15). It does not include the oracles against the nations or the visions, but it does include the oracle against the crooked corn-dealers. Everything else, except for a little exilic material, is allocated to his 'stage B', which is a scribal rather than prophetic work that he dates to the late seventh century, and he emphasizes the entirely different audience, approach, and issues at stake here: the general address to the entire kingdom of Israel, and implicitly to Judah, the condemnation of Bethel, the question of prophetic authority (3.3-8; 7.10-17), the positive ideal of justice, and above all the warning to repent and establish justice, in place of ineluctable condemnation (46-109).

Coote's approach is interesting and important, but I have concluded (Houston 2008: 53) that the difference between condemnation and exhortation cannot be the key to redaction, for the reasons explored above (p. 30), that either genre may function in a context governed by the intention of the other, and that the intentions of prophets (or indeed scribes) are unknown to us. See also Hadjiev 2009: 191-93.

Tchavdar *Hadjiev*, although a thorough redaction critic, is notable for estimating the extent of Amos's own words rather higher than most recent critics, and for returning to Wolff's conviction that early editions of the prophecy of Amos were composed before rather than after the fall of Samaria, in other words that those who collected and handed on Amos's words themselves wished to warn Israel, and not only Judah, of the destiny awaiting it, rather than justifying it after the event. As noted above, like Wolff he sees chaps. 3–6* and chaps. 1–2*, 7–9* as originally separate compositions. He calls 4.1–6.7* the 'Repentance Scroll', with the call to repentance in 5.4-5, 14-15 at its heart (Hadjiev 2009: 179-87), dates it shortly before 722, and defends repentance as a possible object of judgment prophecy (191-93). This 'scroll', he thinks (187-90), was updated in Judah after 722 by adding 3.9-15 and 6.8-14, but most of this material came from Amos. His 'Polemical Scroll' consists of five oracles against the nations, followed by 9.7; 3.3-8*; the five visions; 9.9-10; and 7.10-17 (196); it is intended to state the case against Israel, and then to 'demolish every possible objection which might provide hope...or reason to think that one might evade the judgment'. It is exclusively addressed to Israel, at a time of confidence before 734, or at the time of Hoshea's rebellion c. 725.

The two scrolls were then brought together to form the essence of the present book of Amos, in Judah, probably in the seventh century, with the addition of 1.2; 3.1a, 2; and the hymns, mainly to clarify the structure (198-200). Finally, the book as it is now emerged in the exilic period, again in Judah (205-207). The oracles against Tyre, Edom and Judah; 2.7b, 10-12; 5.25-27; 7.9; 8.3-14; and 9.8-15 were all added at the same editorial stage (201, 203-204). The theological rationale would have been to demonstrate that Israel and Judah had first of all rejected the Law (2.4-5; 6-8), and then the prophets (2.10-12; 3.1-8; 7.10-17 in the context of the visions) (202), which justifies their present condition, sketched in 8.10-14 (106). Hadjiev understands the book as essentially a faithful presentation of the preaching of Amos, yet updated for later situations.

Radine (see also above) attributes a redactional history to the literary-predictive text from the late eighth century that he postulates. There are three main blocks of text that he regards as added to the original eighth-century work (summarized Radine 2010: 170): the oracles against the nations (170-83); the Amaziah narrative (183-97); and the epilogue (9.11-15), which was added last of all, with its eschatological themes shared with other books of the Twelve, particularly Zechariah (198-210).

Amos in the Book of the Twelve

A recent movement, beginning in its present form with James Nogalski (Nogalski 1993), has argued that the book of the Twelve was brought into its present shape as a whole, with particular episodes of redactional activity extending across several of the prophets. It is not possible to devote attention here to all that has been said about Amos in this connection. I will merely note some important conclusions drawn by Nogalski and by Aaron Schart (Schart 1998), together with some remarks by Terence Collins (1993).

Nogalski notes, as have others (e.g. Collins 1993: 65), the use of catchwords at the beginnings and ends of books linking them together. Joel 3.16a (4.16a) is repeated word for word in Amos 1.2a, and the last 18 verses of Joel mention Tyre, Philistia, and Edom, as well as (repeatedly) Zion (Nogalski 1993: 24-25). Obadiah is concerned entirely with Edom, and also refers to 'the nations' (cf. Amos 9.12); the phrase 'from there I will bring you/them down' occurs in both Amos 9.2 and Obad. 4, and Amos 9.13 and Obad. 8 refer to 'mountain(s)' (27-30). This looks impressive, until one realizes that in the LXX Amos is neither preceded by Joel nor followed by Obadiah: in other words until a quite late date the order of the books was not fixed. This makes it less likely that the wording deliberately reflects that of the previous or next book, yet Collins draws the opposite conclusion (1993: 68).

Nogalski's other main positive conclusion is that Hosea, Amos, Micah and Zephaniah, which all have similar superscriptions referring to the reigns of kings (as have Isaiah and Jeremiah), which are often regarded as the result of a Deuteronomistic redaction, were initially transmitted together as a corpus (Nogalski 1993: 278-79), and this is something fairly widely agreed. In this case the LXX supports the idea, with Hosea, Amos and Micah standing together at the start of the Twelve. But Nogalski suggests that other interventions following the same theological agenda, emphasizing the destruction of the kingdoms for their sin, were made across all four books as part of a single plan (279-80).

Schart agrees with all this (1998: 156-233; summary at 305), but develops it in a more speculative direction. He argues that each of the redactional phases of the growth of the book of Amos (he sees six) also involved other books and marked stages in the growth of the corpus. Even before the Deuteronomistic phase, Amos and Hosea shared a common reworking (Schart 1998: 101-155; 305; Jeremias 1996: 41-52).

A somewhat different and much less detailed account of the development of the Book of the Twelve is given by Collins (1993: 62-64). In the case of Amos, he argues that in reading the Twelve through as a book, the place of Joel before Amos has the effect that 'the dire threats against Israel which dominate Amos are softened when read in the light of the more optimistic ending of Joel' (68). Further, it brings two judgments of the 'nations' together (Joel 3(4).1-3 and Amos 1.3–2.3), but the first is followed by the restoration of the fortunes of Israel and Judah, which softens the blow of condemnation of Israel that follows in Amos (69). And the presence of the catchwords already examined shows that this is not an accidental juxtaposition (68).

Conclusions

What verdict should we reach on this whole effort to write the history of the book of Amos? The problem is that the limited evidence is capable of supporting a wide range of theories, as must be quite evident from all the above. If we grant that the extreme views on either hand can be excluded, as has been argued above, we are still left with a very extensive range of views, each of which can point to some evidence in its favour.

It can be said that the evidence supporting redaction is more substantial than the evidence for theories of composition. In other words, while it is relatively certain that some texts do not come from Amos, or do not belong to the earliest composition, it is much less certain how they were brought into the book, and to what extent we can agree on identifying *groups* of additions that belong to a single phase, despite the relatively broad agreement on some points identified above.

Nor is it clear to what extent texts that existed in the earliest written composition, or for that matter any that were added at later stages, go back to Amos. Sayings of Amos could have been handed on among followers or those who heard him before reaching written form many years later, even though it is fair to say that there is no evidence for any formal 'school' (Wolff) or circles of disciples.

It is worth repeating, however, that the book that we have is a literary product, even though it includes material that bears signs of having been intended for oral delivery. It must have been put into shape in a scribal milieu of some kind, where it was given written form, but at the same time taught and passed on orally (cf. Carr 2005).

Further Reading

A general account of the redactional approach to the prophetic books is offered in Collins 1993: 11-36, which concludes with an extensive bibliography up to that date.

All the commentaries deal with the history of the book at greater or less length, or else defend the view that it has no history. The most important commentary from this point of view is Wolff 1977 (esp. 106-13), since not only does he set a benchmark for subsequent work, but he gives some useful, if brief, arguments for his decisions. However, for a thorough but easily comprehensible account giving due weight to all the major views, see Barton 2012: 1-51.

Detailed investigations of the composition and development of the book are offered in the works summarized above, most recently Hadjiev 2009, Radine 2010 and Hamborg 2012: a trio neatly representative of three distinct approaches.

Part III

AMOS READ

Chapter 8

THE RECEPTION AND INFLUENCE OF THE BOOK OF AMOS

We now turn to what is usually known as the 'reception history' of Amos: the way in which, over the centuries, it has been read, interpreted, used in theology, art and literature, and how it has influenced thought and action.

Reading Amos in the Ancient and Medieval Periods

For many centuries the book of Amos does not seem to have attracted any special attention. It was one of the 'minor prophets', and among them seen as less important than the longer books of Hosea and Zechariah. There were a few texts that were seen as important because they were read as foretelling the future of the community, among them 4.13, 5.26-27 and 9.11-12. But what we see as the main thrust of the book, Israel's punishment for social injustice, was not often taken up as a message for contemporaries until modern times.

It has been argued that Isaiah was influenced by Amos's prophecies (Fey 1963), also Jeremiah (Berridge 1979). For example, Isa. 5.11-13 expresses a similar idea to Amos 6.1-7 (but with very few of the same words). But we cannot say that this is a sign of the influence of the *book* of Amos, as we suspect this did not exist in any form until after the fall of Samaria (see above).

The first clear sign of the existence and influence of the book comes with its translation into Greek, probably in the second century BCE, showing that it was known, along with the other prophets of the twelve, in the Jewish community of Alexandria. The translation usually referred to as LXX Amos, best witnessed in the Vatican MS of the Bible ('B' in textual apparatus), is usually fairly literal, but it contains a number of errors (see Gelston 2010: 7*). One of these became important for the early use of the text. At 4.13 it reads 'revealing to people *his* Messiah (*ton Christon autou*)' instead of 'revealing his thoughts' or the like, misreading *mah-ssēḥô* as *mᵉšīḥō* (most of the letters are the same in Hebrew). See below, p. 86.

Amos in the Dead Sea Scrolls

Two texts of Amos, 5.26-27 and 9.11, held great significance for the Qumran community, as seen in the Damascus Document, the community's largely allegorical account of its existence, and in 4Q174 Florilegium, 12-13. 'And all the apostates were given up to the sword, but those who held fast escaped to the land of the north; as God said, *I will exile the tabernacle of your king and the bases of your statues from my tent to Damascus*' (Amos 5.26-27; CD VII.14-15, Vermes 2004: 135). The writer reads *sikkût* as *sukkat*, tabernacle, and *mēhālᵉ'â* 'beyond' as *mē 'ohᵒlî*, 'from my tent'; see Brooke 1980: 400. This is followed by an explanation of the meaning of various expressions in the text, referring to Amos 9.11 for the 'tabernacle'. The exegetical techniques used, which result in an interpretation very far from the straightforward meaning, are explained by George Brooke (Brooke 1980). The Florilegium text also refers to 9.11, saying that 'the fallen tent of David is he who shall arise to save Israel' (Vermes 2004: 526). Brooke argues that in the CD passage the Amos text and Num. 24.17 are interpreted as prophecies of the coming of two Messiahs, those 'of Israel' and 'of Aaron'.

Amos in the New Testament

It is just the same two passages of Amos that are referred to in the New Testament's only two identifiable quotations from the book. In Stephen's long diatribe in Acts 7 on the people's history of apostasy, the story of the golden calf is linked with Amos 5.26-27 (Acts 7.42-43), which he argues shows how God abandoned the idolaters to exile beyond Babylon, substituting that name for 'Damascus' in the quotation. Unlike the Qumran scribe, he interprets the text in its straightforward sense. Amos 9.11-12 appears a few chapters later, in the account of the council at Jerusalem, where James quotes it to show that 'the words of the prophets' foretold the conversion of the Gentiles (Acts 15.16-17). The LXX text is quoted, where v. 12 is read differently from the Hebrew, 'that the rest of humankind may seek the Lord and all the nations over whom my name has been called'. (The translator reads *'dm* as *'ādām* rather than *ᵉdôm* and *ydršw*, they seek, instead of *yyršw*, they possess. See Gelston 2010: 88*.) It is notable that in both places Amos is not named: the quotations are simply representative of 'the prophets'. Taken together one might suggest that the two quotations sum up the story Luke wishes to tell in Acts: because Israel has rejected God's salvation, the apostles turn, under God's guidance, to the Gentiles. This has been foretold by 'the prophets', and is therefore God's plan.

Amos in Rabbinic Literature

'The Rabbis read the book of Amos like the other witnesses to the prophetic tradition, phrase by phrase, word by word, scarcely troubling themselves to discover the original import of Amos's message or to put it in its original context' (Martin-Achard 1984: 198, my translation). This is entirely true, but states no more than one would expect: the purpose of reading Scripture was to edify present-day believers.

The only continuous reading of Amos in ancient Jewish tradition is in the Aramaic translation, Targum Jonathan on the Minor Prophets (see Cathcart and Gordon 1989: 75-96). The Targum often paraphrases, but 'only occasionally' has a 'substantial interpretative expansion' (Gelston 2010: 9*). One or two of these are interesting, however. Amos's final vision in 9.1-2 is developed extensively in order to apply it to Judaean history: 'I saw the glory of the Lord; it ascended by the cherub and rested on the altar; and he said, "If my people Israel will not return to the law, extinguish the lamp; king Josiah shall be slain, the temple shall be laid waste, and the temple courts shall be destroyed; and the vessels of the Sanctuary shall be taken into captivity"' (Cathcart and Gordon 1989: 94, with nn. 2, 3).

There appear to be approximately 200 references to Amos in the Talmud and Midrashim (see Neusner 2007). If this seems a large number, it has to be measured against the vast extent of these collections. Neusner quotes each reference with its sometimes extensive context in the rabbinic source. Generally they are quoted as proof texts in discussions, without reference to their biblical context, to support a ruling or interpretation. Rabbi Abahu, however, interprets Amos 3.2 for its own sake, with a parable: he says it is 'like a man who lent money to two people, one a friend, the other an enemy. From the friend he collects the money little by little, from the enemy he collects all at once' (b. *Abodah Zarah* 4a; Neusner 2007: 108). The text is interpreted in a way that respects the Jewish conviction of election, and this changes its contextual meaning, in which Israel is to suffer at least as severely as other nations.

A famous passage in the Babylonian Talmud (b. *Makkoth* 23b-24a; Neusner 2007: 105-107) discusses how various passages in scripture reduce the number of the 613 commandments of the Torah. Amos 5.4 comes at the very end: 'Amos came and reduced them to a single one, as it is said, "For thus says the Lord to the house of Israel, Seek me and live".' This single commandment covers them all.

Martin-Achard (1984: 198) comments that the rabbis interpreted in accordance with their own theology, but that in spite of their ethical emphasis they failed to capture the 'tragic note' of Amos's intervention to proclaim the end of Israel. But of course they were not trying to present the message of Amos for its own sake. Such a message would have been utterly irrelevant and even abhorrent to the faithful and persecuted people among whom they worked.

Amos in Early and Medieval Christianity

In ancient and medieval Christian thought the prophets are seen primarily as advance witnesses to Christ. This is evident in the way in which Amos is used. J.G. Kelly offers some statistics, quoted by Martin-Achard (1984: 201-2), on citations from Amos in patristic literature. In the selected literature, there are 204 citations, which cover exactly half (73) of the verses of the book. No fewer than 23 are of 4.13, which, as we saw above, is in the LXX an explicitly Messianic prophecy, 'revealing to people his Christ (or 'anointed one'). There are also 23 citations of 8.11, perhaps less predictably. It enables writers to spiritualize ideas of fasting.

Besides citations in general literature, several patristic writers wrote commentaries on Amos, including Cyril of Alexandria, Theodore of Mopsuestia and Theodoret of Cyrus in Greek, and Jerome in Latin. For these interpreters of the fifth century CE, the prophecy of Amos demonstrates how God made clear from remote antiquity his plan to save the world through Christ and his church. We have seen that the book justifies the 'end' of Israel and its replacement by Davidic Judah (9.11-12). It requires very little artifice to re-interpret this scheme as the story of the rejection of the Jews and the calling in their place of the Church, and this is in effect what these exegetes do. They are of course assisted by the way in which the book is used in Acts (see above).

Cyril, for example, applies the condemnation of 5.21-22 to the worship of the Jews and the heretics, while asserting that God gladly receives the spiritual worship of true believers. Verse 24 is then treated as the threat of judgment demanding repentance. (The LXX text of 5.24 means 'and judgment will roll down like water, and righteousness like an unfordable torrent', and Jerome's Vulgate Latin translation 'and judgment will be revealed like water, and justice like a mighty torrent'.) Then when Cyril comes to the end of the book, he offers a brief summary of Second Temple history as a literal interpretation of 9.11-12 and 13-15, but then in each case launches into a much more elaborate allegorical reading. 'The inner and truer interpretation would apply to Christ', he says of 11-12, reading it as a prophecy of the general resurrection—the 'raising up of the booth' of the flesh (cf. Jn 1.14; 2 Cor. 5.1) and (as in Acts) the coming of the Gentiles to Christ. The 'more spiritual' understanding of vv. 13-15 is then as a prophecy of the Church's production of spiritual fruits. (Cyril, *Comm. on Amos* 53; 84-85 [PG 71: 505-508; 575-82])

Jerome's interpretation is similar; but he allegorizes more comprehensively, and often without allowing the literal sense as an alternative; and his comments have a much sharper anti-Jewish tone. If God were to accept the sacrifices of those who shouted 'Crucify him!', it would be like accepting the offering of Cain (5.21-22); but he will accept our gifts, as he accepted Abel's (1969: 294-95). The final verses of the book are seen as prophesying the rise of the Church and the conversion of all nations (9.11-12). The Church will be firmly planted, never to be uprooted (9.15), though shaken with persecutions; attacked but not overcome (1969: 347-48).

The aspect of Amos which is most prominent to us, its denunciation of social injustice, is rarely applied to present-day evils in the patristic writers. Andrew Mein notes that we do find this to some extent in Cyril (Mein 2011: 120), who illustrates his exegesis of 2.6-7 with a large number of quotations from the Old Testament recommending justice and mercy, and eventually uses the first person plural: '*We* seriously offend God when we exploit the weak and "strike the lowly with our fists", as Scripture says [Isa. 58.4], embittering with our hostility those who are burdened by poverty, when we ought rather to extend to them the hand of love' (Cyril, *PG* 71: 411; 2007: 31).

Mein goes on to note that 'justice and politics come increasingly to the fore in the medieval period'. Beryl Smalley notes how Archbishop Stephen Langton (c. 1150–1228) compares Amaziah to a worldly prelate of his own day, and Amos to a scholar 'fresh from Paris' (as Langton had been) who comes and preaches justice, and is told 'leave my bishopric or my parish, return to your studies at Paris, "eat bread and prophesy there", confine your teaching and preaching to Paris' (Smalley 1931: 72-73). Another source of such thought, according to Mein, is Nicholas of Lyra (c. 1270–1340) in his *Postilla moralis* (1331–39). Interpreting 'Israel' in 2.6 as 'seeing God' and therefore as the clergy, he describes 'typical clerical sins: lust and greed', which 'lead to the perversion of justice'. Amaziah, as in Langton, represents wicked priests who prevent preachers from speaking out. Mein comments that Nicholas's interpretations 'reflect an awareness of the church's failure to establish justice, and of the fact that Amos offers preachers a resource with which to address the abuses they encounter in both the secular and the ecclesiastical realms' (Mein 2011: 122).

Savonarola

The first writer or preacher who systematically expounds Amos in relation to social and political abuses of his day is Girolamo Savonarola, the Dominican friar, Prior of St Mark's at Florence, who launched an attempt, during the confusion following the French invasion and the downfall of the Medici in late 1494, to shape Florence into a Christian republic as he conceived it, and dominated the city until his enemies succeeded in having him executed in March 1498. In Lent 1496 he preached every day in the Cathedral, first on Amos and then on Zechariah. Zechariah would have appealed to his strongly apocalyptic imagination. His reason for choosing Amos, as Mein suggests, is that it 'combines forthright condemnation of the powerful with serious reflection on the prophetic role' (Mein 2011: 126), and both were central to his conception of his own role and calling in Florence.

He himself, he believed, was called to a prophetic ministry, and effectively identifies himself with the Old Testament prophet. So on Amos 3.8 he comments:

> Amos, prophesying against those who did not want to believe him and were saying 'Don't prophesy' [2.12], answers 'The lion has roared, who will not fear? The Lord God has spoken, who will not prophesy?' So I say to you: You don't want me to preach, you don't want me to prophesy; the lion, I say, is roaring; the Lord's will is so-and-so, and who is there who ought not to obey the Lord who has spoken it?... Why do you not want me to obey the Eternal Father? (Savonarola 1971: I, 285-86, my translation).

Savonarola makes the same interpretative move here as many modern scholars, understanding Amos as replying to an objection by his hearers. But Savonarola sees himself as the prophet whom the powerful are attempting to silence.

A few days earlier he had preached on Amos 2.6-8. He first gave a brief literal exposition, and then two extensive 'spiritual' readings, employing analogy to apply the text to contemporary circumstances. He is scathing on the corruption of the clergy. The 'fourth' and worst sin of the clergy, after pride, greed and lust, is setting a bad example to their flocks. This is encouraged by the sale of benefices, a notorious scandal in fifteenth-century Italy. Savonarola represents God as saying:

> You have sold the poor man for sandals, that is, for a cheap thing, because you put a higher price on dogs, mules and horses than on my poor, whom I have redeemed with my blood, and you have let him die of hunger (Savonarola 1971: I, 193, my translation).

He moves on through the text, naturally applying 'father and son...' (2.7) to the sexual immorality of the clergy, especially in Rome; while the 'pledged garments' (2.8) (*robba* = both 'garment' and 'property' [Mein 2011: 131]) represent the property which the corrupt clergy ought to distribute to the poor, but instead give to their lackeys and spend on their mules and horses (I, 195).

Savonarola's political concerns lead him to devote two sermons to the application of this text to the 'princes' or 'tyrants' who ruled many Italian states at the time, and from whom Florence had recently been delivered to create a broadly based republican government strongly promoted by himself (Mein 2011: 129). One effect of tyranny is the corruption of justice, which Savonarola sees referred to in 2.6, and the subjection of all public officials to the tyrant's will.

Thus Savonarola reads himself, his situation and his opponents into the book of Amos, and the oppressed poor of Israel become the oppressed poor of Florence, exploited for the sake of the pride, greed and ambition of both clergy and politicians. It will not be for some centuries that another such powerfully personal reading emerges. In part this had to wait for the new understanding of prophecy developed by historical-critical scholarship in the later 19th century.

The Reformers

Both Luther (1483–1546) and Calvin (1509–1564), who were above all biblical exegetes, comment on the whole Bible, and therefore also on Amos. They aim primarily at expounding the literal sense of the text in the historical context as they understand it, but this does not deter them from applying it to current affairs as they see fit, and particularly from attacking their religious adversaries.

Thus, for Luther (*Praelectiones in prophetas minores* [WA 13: 124-206], 1524–25), Amos 5 is about justification by faith. God is to be sought (5.4) by faith rather than by works. 'He [God] does not want us to imitate the fathers' deeds but their faith.' On 5.21: 'God wants to be served by faith, not otherwise'. He refers 5.24 to the coming Gospel, when justice 'will fall like an irresistible torrent, the justice of God.' (Martin-Achard 1984: 224). The episode with Amaziah, on the other hand, he compares to the confrontation of Protestants with the Pope.

Likewise Calvin, whose lectures on Amos were given in 1557, naturally understands the 'plain sense' of the text in the light of his own theology: so when God exhorted the people to 'seek me and live' (5.4), this did not have the same effect with everyone; 'for the Lord inwardly attracted his elect, and others were rendered inexcusable' (Calvin 1846: 253).

He takes the opportunity of Amos' frequent ironic dismissal of the sacrificial worship of Israel to denounce the superstition of the 'Papists' (187, 193, 289, 348, etc.). More deeply felt is his denunciation of their suppression of 'the liberty of prophesying' (195, on 2.12). 'The word of God is repudiated when the freedom of teaching is restrained'. His most powerful reflections on this issue come in his exposition of the Amaziah episode (7.10-17). God's servants need to be prepared for conflict and death, but just as prepared for the insidious flattery of their enemies, which he detects in Amaziah's words (344-45). Amaziah was particularly anxious that Amos should leave Bethel, whatever he did in Judah, and Calvin compares this to Rome's need to hang on to France, Spain and Italy, while being content to let Germany go for the time being. But on the words 'because it is the king's sanctuary', he becomes most passionate against the subordination of the church to the state typical especially of England, noting that Bishop Gardiner, before becoming Mary's chancellor, had defended the measures of Henry VIII on the grounds that the king can order religion as he pleases in his own realm (348-50).

Calvin is more sparing of contemporary references for the exposition of Amos's social criticism; however, on 5.12 he notes how common it was in his day for judges to expect bribes (269); and on 8.4-6 he denounces the common custom of hoarding grain in the expectation of a price rise.

The rejection of allegory distinguishing Reformation from ancient and medieval interpretation is seen most clearly at the end of the book. Calvin states confidently on 9.11 that 'it is certain that the Prophet here refers to the advent of Christ' (405); yet goes on to interpret vv. 13-15 largely literally, until a very brief closing comment that 'Christ's kingdom abounds in spiritual blessings' (408-13).

The Historical-critical Revolution

As I have said, the general adoption of Amos as *the* prophet of social justice had to wait on the revolution in the understanding of the prophets worked by the late-19th century German critics (cf. Martin-Achard 1984: 243). Wellhausen, in his epoch-making *Prolegomena to the History of Israel* (1878: Wellhausen 1957), showed that the eighth-century prophets owed nothing to the priestly code in the Pentateuch, which in an argument largely still accepted by critical scholars he pronounced to be of post-exilic origin; while contrariwise the prophets had influenced Deuteronomy especially, but also to some extent the older narrative sources of the Pentateuch, J and E. And Amos was the earliest of them, which made Amos effectively the originator of what is most distinctive of Old Testament religion, summed up in the phrase 'ethical monotheism'. (A complete list of the 61 references to the book of Amos in Wellhausen 1957 can be found at Clifford 2011: 141 n. 2.) Most characteristic here is the attack on the value placed on the cult by contrast with justice (Wellhausen 1957: 23, 47-48). This was the root of a totally new approach to religion, 'independent of all traditional and preconceived human opinions' (48).

Even before the publication of *Prolegomena*, a similar thesis had been advanced by Bernhard Duhm (1875), as indicated in his title ('The theology of the prophets as the basis of the inner history of the development of the Israelite religion'). The new approach was popularized in English-speaking countries by S.R. Driver and William Robertson Smith, among others. Smith devoted a series of public lectures as early as 1882 to the new point of view on the early prophets, emphasizing their independence of the Law. On Amos he says, 'the sin of Israel is not merely that it has broken through laws of right and wrong patent to all mankind, but that it has refused to listen to these laws as they were personally explained to it by the Judge Himself' (Smith 2002: 138). That is, not in the Pentateuchal laws, but in the 'personal converse' of 'Jehovah' with Israel. He goes on, '[Jehovah] is not to be found by sacrifice, for in it he takes no pleasure; what Jehovah requires of those who seek him is the practice of civil righteousness' (139). 'The sinners of Israel [9.10] are the corrupt rulers and their associates, the unjust and sensual oppressors, the men who have no regard to civil righteousness' (142). He makes no reference to Christ in his brief exposition of 9.11-15 (142-43).

Thus a wide audience became familiar with a view of Amos quite different from the traditional one. He was not a preacher of the Mosaic Law, but of a universal morality. His God was concerned above all with 'civil righteousness', and those he called sinners, who would be destroyed along with their state, were guilty of social oppression. He was not a long-range prophet of the coming of Christ, but was concerned with the immediate threat of destruction. The restoration of Israel did also come within his purview according to Smith's view, but, as we have seen (p. 30), Wellhausen dismissed the final verses as secondary.

Amos as Inspiration in Struggles for Social Justice

As this view spread and became standard, being taught in universities and theological colleges and given in popular guides to the Bible, the way was open to gain inspiration from the book for present-day struggles against social oppression. An early example of this influence was Walter Rauschenbusch, one of the leaders of the so-called 'Social Gospel' movement in America, whose *Christianity and the Social Crisis* (Rauschenbusch 1912) begins with a chapter on the Hebrew Prophets.

It is no coincidence that it is just at this time that we find lay people, neither clergy nor biblical scholars, beginning to acknowledge Amos, among the other Old Testament prophets, as an inspiration in their struggles for social justice in their own society. An example is Ben Tillett, the British labour leader (1860–1943). According to W.H. Bennett (Bennett 1908: 356; see Tomes 2015: 283 [=2004: 300]), the writings on the prophets of Archibald Duff, the somewhat maverick Old Testament scholar who taught at Yorkshire Independent College, provided him with inspiration—as one may well believe if one glances at Duff's vivid account of Amos (Duff 1891: 35-89; see Tomes 2015: 298-301 or 2004: 281-84).

Since the early twentieth century appeal has constantly been made to Amos, among other prophets, as model or inspiration in the struggle for justice, despite the fact that biblical scholars have repeatedly pointed out (assuming that the prophet Amos is the source of the main body of the text) that he cannot be regarded as a reformer or a revolutionary, since he saw no future for Israel. No matter: the standard by which he judged Israel was 'justice and righteousness'; and of course 5.24 is taken as the key verse, invariably interpreted as an exhortation; all other possible interpretations are overlooked.

It is possible to trace two main strands in the modern appropriation of Amos. One lays emphasis on the ethical aspect of the book, its call for 'justice and righteousness', and tends to interpret its judgment prophecy in effect as an implicit call for repentance and reform: certainly this is how it actually uses it in its application to contemporary society. This is the predominant emphasis in texts that locate themselves within contemporary society and apply Amos to it.

The other strand stresses the aspect of inexorable judgment. Karl Barth, for example, ends his study of Amos in his *Church Dogmatics* (Barth 1958: 445-52) by pronouncing that '[God] maintains the covenant by placing the inhumanity of man under his merciless denunciation and the judgment which remorselessly engulfs it' (452). This approach also can be seen, though less commonly, in interpretations expressing engagement with contemporary society and politics.

A couple of examples only of each approach will suffice. More can be found in Carroll R. 2002: 26-30, 53-72.

One of the most influential preachers and political campaigners of the second half of the twentieth century was Martin Luther King, and he placed a deep reliance in his preaching, more so than in his published works, according to Russell Bartlett (Bartlett 1993), on the text, themes and example of the Hebrew prophets and in particular on Amos. Bartlett describes Amos 5.24 as 'easily King's favorite verse from either testament' (10), and refers to sermons from 1955, 1965 and 1968 that employ both characteristic themes of the prophets and a prophetic model of preaching (cf. Carroll R. 2002: 57-58). Like Savonarola, King saw himself as called to a prophetic ministry on the model of the Hebrew prophets (Bartlett 1993: 28-30, 35): the difference is that he also saw other ministers and indeed all Christians in the same role. The latter two sermons not only quote the prophets, including Amos 5.24, but directly discuss their relevance to the campaigns against racism, poverty and militarism in which King was involved. King, who though a radical was no revolutionary, clearly understood 5.24, and hence Amos as a whole, as an exhortation and a warning to the people of the United States to establish justice.

King's assassination in April 1968 occurred only a few months before the World Council of Churches held its fourth assembly at Uppsala; he had been scheduled to preach at the assembly's opening service. According to Hans-Ruedi Weber's account (Weber 1977: 224-27), it was decided to add an extra session on 'White racism or world community', in which the American black writer James Baldwin challenged the churches to action rather than mere words; and the same evening a dramatic presentation was given, written by Olaf Hartmann and entitled 'On That Day', and consisting of a ballet on the life and message of Amos, a rare example of the reception of Amos in a work of art, apart from his presence in series of carved or stained glass figures of the prophets. According to Weber, the concurrence of these events led directly to the decision to launch the Programme to Combat Racism, one of the most controversial—but prophetic!—projects of the WCC.

Unlike most other appropriations of Amos, Carroll R.'s study of the book in the Latin American context (Carroll R. 1992) focuses primarily on its view of the religion of Israel, and is not applied only to the oppressive elite. Amos presents a complex, a 'world', of overlapping practices that between them involve the whole population and function to validate the social and political setup (209; see above, pp. 27, 34, 39). And it is also true in Latin America that religion is a 'world' of various practices and beliefs, but a number of significant symbols are shared by the great majority of the population. 'Both right and left, Protestant and Roman Catholic, indeed all of Latin America's Christian society and movements, must come under the scrutinizing light of the divine demand represented in the church's "classic" text' (281). Carroll R.'s concern was that among Christians who supported the radical left (with which he certainly has sympathy), a particular political option was being identified as 'God's own', and 'the demand of allegiance [made] absolute' (295), so that it falls under the same judgment as the state-supporting religion of Israel (299). I have criticized the exegetical base of this view above, but the application may be justified even so.

Turning to more severe interpretations, Carroll R. notes the words of the Argentinian liberation theologian J. Severino Croatto, in a Spanish-language journal, but taking up his study of Amos 9.11-15 in Croatto 1987: 55-56, which points out that this hopeful conclusion to the book could only be added *after* the inevitable judgment had been experienced, but it then transformed the meaning of the earlier oracles of judgment. 'Israel will not be converted by the prophetical denunciation; it will be converted in the suffering of its downfall' (Croatto 1987: 56). But in the same way, he says in his later article, reconciliation and forgiveness should only have been offered to the Argentinian military for their torture and murder of dissidents *after* the law had taken its due course (Carroll R. 2002: 28).

Liberation theologians in general have tended to work more from Exodus than from the prophets. This is exemplified in a significant way in the work of the Mexican scholar and adviser to grassroots groups José Miranda (Miranda 1977). He starts from a question posed by Würthwein, which Miranda describes as the most important exegetical question that can be asked:

> But what is the meaning of the fact that Amos exposes interhuman injustices? In the last analysis these are crimes which occur among all the peoples of the world in the most varied circumstances; and we always end up by finding a *modus vivendi* with them without too much squeamishness. Is not Amos assigning them too much importance when he sees in them the

cause of the great approaching disaster? (Würthwein 1950: 47, as translated
in Miranda 1977: 160).

Würthwein's answer is that these crimes are forbidden in the Law (see
above, p. 40). But Miranda points out that there is no reference to any law
in Amos or the other (eighth-century) prophets. Rather, both the laws and
the prophets' denunciations are based in the tradition of the Exodus. The
legal compromises that allow slavery (Exod. 21.2-6 and Deut. 15.12-18)
are incompatible with Amos 2.6 and 8.6. 'According to Amos, even this
compromise cannot be reconciled with the Yahweh who broke into history
to release the slaves' (158). Miranda here overlooks that Amos does not say
anything about Yhwh releasing Israel from slavery; perhaps, basing himself
in Exodus, he assumes that it is implied in 2.10, 3.1 and 9.7.

That still leaves Würthwein's question unanswered. Miranda's answer
is that Israel was chosen to teach the world justice (he derives this from a
strained exegesis of Gen. 18.19 [94-96]), so that to accept injustice in their
society like all the others is 'a betrayal of all the human beings who have
suffered and are suffering' (169). The justice of God, taught by Amos and
revealed in Christ, is 'in absolute contrast with the justice of human civilization and law, in which sin has been incarnated' (192). This is the sharpest
possible rejection of the 'reformist' understanding of Amos, making Amos
the enemy of 'human civilization and law'.

The Hermeneutic of Suspicion

While all the interpretations and appropriations studied so far have treated
the book positively as a source of truth and inspiration, many viewing it
theologically as the word of God, quite a number of recent writers have
adopted a more suspicious viewpoint, often taking up the standpoint of
those neglected or criticized in the book, and questioning the validity of its
denunciations.

Feminist Interpretation

The most widespread variety of this approach appears in the writings of
feminist interpreters. The general criticism of the whole Bible made by
them is that it accepts the patriarchal character of society, in that it is run
by and for men, and that its texts as a result tend to be 'androcentric', that
is, centred on men. This is no less true of Amos.

Judith E. Sanderson's brief commentary on Amos in *The Women's Bible
Commentary* (Sanderson 1992) recognizes the truth of Amos's denunciations of the oppression of the poor, but points to several blind spots. Amos
speaks exclusively of poor *men* as suffering from oppression (see above,
p. 36, and Bird 1997) and says not a word about the oppression of women,

apart from the single reference to 'the girl' in 2.7, of whom Sanderson says 'On one interpretation, the girl [has] got lost in the theological accusation' (208). Unlike other prophets, Amos never mentions widows as oppressed. Yet in most societies, including modern Western ones, women suffer disproportionately from poverty. Women otherwise appear in Amos as subject to judgment, in 4.1-3 and 7.17. Amaziah's wife and children's fate is pronounced as a punishment for him; they are treated as mere appendages whose suffering is ignored. Although the understanding of the phrase 'cows of Bashan' as insulting has been 'imported into the passage by commentators' (209), Sanderson sees this passage as scapegoating women for injustices that have been created and maintained by men. 'A survey of modern commentaries on Amos 4.1 reveals the alacrity with which women are blamed for societies' evils, and their relative powerlessness is disregarded' (205-06). It can be seen that Sanderson is as critical of Amos's commentators as of Amos: a point taken up by Clines (1995: 77; see below).

Carol J. Dempsey's criticisms of Amos (Dempsey 2000: 7-21) go rather deeper than Sanderson's, into the book's portrayal of God. The picture of the male warrior God, who 'sends fire on the walls' of rebellious cities, who deals with injustice by destroying the oppressors and their whole nation, is derived from 'the experiences and ideologies' of warfare, and is of a piece with the patriarchal character of Israel's society and its experience of hierarchy. The text takes for granted that some people have power over others, and may abuse it, but that God has power over all. But when God's power is used to punish an entire nation for the guilt of its rulers, that is a further injustice (11).

Metacommentating Amos

David Clines's lively critical essay on Amos commentaries (Clines 1995) objects to their method on the grounds that while purporting to describe the text from a critical scholarly point of view, they adopt its viewpoint and ideology without telling the reader that that is what they are doing. Thus they describe the social situation by adopting the text's partisan view of it, often with rhetorical flourishes (e.g.: 'They make their lords (husbands) the instruments of their own desire, ruling the society of Israel from behind the scenes with sweet petulant nagging for wealth to support their indolent dalliance. The power behind the corrupt courts (5.10f.) and odious business practices (8.4ff.) is theirs'—Mays 1969: 72.) When it comes to the judgment, Clines seemingly accepts the force of Würthwein's question (above), without having an answer. '[The commentators] *agree* with Amos that both Israel and the surrounding nations *deserve to be punished*, and that such punishment should be *capital*' (Clines 1995: 90, italics original).

> It is…awful to ascribe the destruction of a state and the forceable [*sic*]
> deportation of its citizens to an avenging God. If that is how a believer finds
> himself or herself impelled to conclude, that it is a terrible thing to fall into
> the hands of the living God, the metacommentator can respect that. But to
> affirm it casually, to pretend that it is unproblematic—*that* is not scholarly,
> it is not even human (92).

It will be seen that Clines's criticism of commentators is rooted in a concern
about the stance of the text itself that I would share (see pp. 47-48).

Further Reading

The most comprehensive guide to the reception of the book of Amos, is,
for anyone who can read French, Martin-Achard 1984: 161-270, 297-301.

In English there may eventually be a volume, or part of a volume, on
Amos in the Blackwell Bible Commentaries Through the Centuries series;
but it is not announced. For particular periods, see:

Neusner 2007 for the rabbinic literature. The texts are arranged in the
order of the sources. There is an index of Amos verses, but it has several
omissions.

Ferreiro 2003: 83-116, for the patristic period. But it is of limited use.
He gives a single passage on each verse, commenting on a great variety of
topics, but no clear overview of the character of patristic interpretation such
as I have tried to give above.

A volume on the Twelve, not yet published, in the series Reformation
Commentary on Scripture, for the Reformation.

Mein 2011 treats late medieval interpretation as an introduction to his
study of Savonarola.

Carroll R. 2002: 53-72 is a survey, illustrated by excerpts, of recent
contextual interpretation, and he includes works interpreting Amos with
suspicion.

BIBLIOGRAPHY

Abbott, H. Porter
    2008   *The Cambridge Introduction to Narrative* (Cambridge: Cambridge University Press, 2nd edn).
Ahn, John J., and Stephen L. Cook (eds.)
    2009   *Thus Says the Lord: Essays on the Former and Latter Prophets in Honor of Robert R. Wilson* (LHBOTS, 502; New York/London: T. & T. Clark).
Alter, Robert
    1985   *The Art of Biblical Poetry* (New York: Basic Books).
    1987   'The Characteristics of Ancient Hebrew Poetry', in R. Alter and F. Kermode (eds.), *The Literary Guide to the Bible* (London: Fontana): 611-24.
Andersen, Francis I., and David Noel Freedman
    1989   *Amos: A New Translation with Introduction and Commentary* (AB, 24A; New York: Doubleday).
Auld, A. Graeme
    1983   'Prophets through the Looking Glass: Between Writings and Moses', *JSOT* 27: 3-23. Reprinted in Gordon (ed.) 1995: 289-307.
    1986   *Amos* (Old Testament Guides; Sheffield: Sheffield Academic Press).
Austin, J.L.
    1975   *How to Do Things with Words* (Oxford: Clarendon Press, 2nd edn).
Austin, Steven A., Gordon W. Franz and Eric G. Frost
    2000   'Amos's Earthquake: An Extraordinary Middle East Seismic Event of 750 B.C.', *International Geology Review* 42(7): 657-71.
Bach, Robert
    1957   'Gottesrecht und weltliches Recht in der Verkündigung des Amos', in W. Schneemelcher (ed.), *Festschrift für Günther Dehn* (Neukirchen–Vluyn: Neukirchener Verlag): 23-34.
Barstad, Hans M.
    1984   *The Religious Polemics of Amos: Studies in the Preaching of Am 2, 7B-8; 4,1-13; 5,1-27; 6, 4-7; 8, 14* (Leiden: E.J. Brill).
Barth, Karl
    1958   *The Doctrine of Reconciliation (Church Dogmatics, Volume IV, 2)* (trans. G.W. Bromiley; Edinburgh: T. & T. Clark).
Bartlett, Russell S.
    1993   'Let Justice Roll Down Like Waters: The Model of Hebrew Prophecy in the Ministry of Martin Luther King, Jr.', *Journal of the Interdenominational Theological Center* 21: 10-38.
Barton, John
    1979   'Natural Law and Poetic Justice in the Old Testament', *JTS* 30: 1-14.
    1980   *Amos's Oracles against the Nations: A Study of Amos 1:3–2:5* (Society for Old Testament Study Monograph Series, 6; Cambridge: Cambridge University Press).

1990   'History and Rhetoric in the Prophets', in M. Warner (ed.), *The Bible as Rhet-
        oric: Studies in Biblical Persuasion and Credibility* (Warwick Studies in Phi-
        losophy and Literature; London: Routledge): 51-64.
2003   *Understanding Old Testament Ethics: Approaches and Explorations* (Louis-
        ville, KY: Westminster/John Knox Press).
2005   'The Prophets and the Cult', in John Day (ed.), *Temple and Worship in Bib-
        lical Israel* (LHBOTS, 422; London/New York: T. & T. Clark International):
        111-22.
2009   'Prophecy and Theodicy', in Ahn and Cook (eds.) 2009: 73-86.
2012   *The Theology of the Book of Amos* (Old Testament Theology; Cambridge/
        New York: Cambridge University Press).
2014   *Ethics in Ancient Israel* (Oxford: Oxford University Press).

Ben Zvi, Ehud
2003   'The Prophetic Book: A Key Form of Prophetic Literature', in Marvin A.
        Sweeney and Ben Zvi (eds.), *The Changing Face of Form Criticism for the
        Twenty-first Century* (Grand Rapids: Eerdmans): 276-97.

Ben Zvi, Ehud
2005   *Hosea* (The Forms of the Old Testament Literature, XXIA/1; Grand Rapids,
        MI and Cambridge, UK: Eerdmans).

Bendor, S.
1996   *The Social Structure of Ancient Israel: The Institution of the Family (Beit
        'Ab) from the Settlement to the End of the Monarchy* (Jerusalem Biblical
        Studies, 7; Jerusalem: Simor).

Bennett, W.H.
1908   'Survey of Recent Literature on Old Testament Theology', *Review of Theol-
        ogy and Philosophy* 4: 349-56.

Berquist, Jon L.
1993   'Dangerous Waters of Justice and Righteousness: Amos 5:18-27', *BTB* 23:
        54-63.

Berridge, John Maclennan
1979   'Jeremias und die Prophetie des Amos', *TZ* 36: 321-41.

Bird, Phyllis
1997   'Poor Man or Poor Woman: Gendering the Poor in Prophetic Texts', in
        Bird, *Missing Persons and Mistaken Identities: Women and Gender in
        Ancient Israel* (Minneapolis: Fortress Press): 67-78; repr. from B. Becking
        and M. Dijkstra (eds.), *On Reading Prophetic Texts: Gender-Specific and
        Related Studies in Memory of Fokkelien van Dijk-Hemmes* (Leiden: E.J.
        Brill, 1996): 37-51.

Blenkinsopp, Joseph
2003   'Bethel in the Neo-Babylonian Period', in Oded Lipschits and Joseph Blen-
        kinsopp (eds.), *Judah and the Judeans in the Neo-Babylonian Period* (Winona
        Lake, IN: Eisenbrauns): 93-107.

Boecker, Hans Jochen
1981   'Überlegungen zur Kultpolemik der vorexilischen Propheten', in Jeremias
        and Perlitt (eds.): 169-80.

Boer, Roland
2015   *The Sacred Economy of Ancient Israel* (Library of Ancient Israel; Louisville,
        KY: Westminster/John Knox Press).

Brooke, George J.
    1980   'The Amos-Numbers (CD 7,13b–8,1a) and Messianic Expectation', *ZAW* 92:
            397-404.
Brueggemann, Walter
    1997   *Theology of the Old Testament; Testimony, Dispute, Advocacy* (Minneapolis:
            Fortress Press).
Calvin, John
    1846   *Commentaries on the Twelve Minor Prophets* (trans. John Owen; Edinburgh:
    (1559) Calvin Translation Society): II, 147-413.
Carr, David M.
    2005   *Writing on the Tablet of the Heart: Origins of Scripture and Literature* (New
            York: Oxford University Press).
Carroll R., Mark Daniel
    1992   *Contexts for Amos: Prophetic Poetics in Latin American Perspective* (JSOT-
            Sup, 132; Sheffield: Sheffield Academic Press).
    1995   'Reflecting on War and Utopia in the Book of Amos: The Relevance of a
            Literary Reading of the Prophetic Text for Central America', in Carroll R.,
            David J.A. Clines and Philip R. Davies (eds.), *The Bible in Human Soci-
            ety: Essays in Honour of John Rogerson* (JSOTSup, 200; Sheffield: Sheffield
            Academic Press): 105-21.
    2002   *Amos—The Prophet and His Oracles: Research on the Book of Amos* (Louis-
            ville, KY; Westminster/John Knox Press).
Carroll, Robert
    1983   'Poets not Prophets: A Response to "Prophets through the Looking Glass"',
            JSOT 27: 25-31.
Cathcart, Kevin J., and R.P. Gordon (ed. and trans.)
    1989   *The Targum of the Minor Prophets* (The Bible in Aramaic, 14; Edinburgh:
            T. & T. Clark).
Chaney, Marvin L.
    1986   'Systemic Study of the Israelite Monarchy', *Semeia* 37: 53-76.
    1993   'Bitter Bounty: The Dynamics of Political Economy Critiqued by the Eighth-
            Century Prophets', in Norman K. Gottwald and Richard Horsley (eds.), *The
            Bible and Liberation: Political and Social Hermeneutics*, rev. edn (Mary-
            knoll, NY: Orbis Books and London: SPCK): 250-63.
Clements, R.E.
    1965   *Prophecy and Covenant* (London: SCM Press).
Clifford, Hywel
    2011   'Amos in Wellhausen's *Prolegomena*', in Hagedorn and Mein 2011: 141-56.
Clines, David J.A.
    1995   'Metacommentating Amos', in *Interested Parties: The Ideology of Writers
            and Readers of the Hebrew Bible* (JSOTSup, 235; Sheffield: Sheffield Aca-
            demic Press): 76-93.
Coggins, Richard James
    2000   *Joel and Amos* (NCBC; Sheffield: Sheffield Academic Press).
Collins, Terence (Terry)
    1993   *The Mantle of Elijah: The Redaction Criticism of the Prophetic Books* (The
            Biblical Seminar, 20; Sheffield: JSOT Press).
Cook, H.J.
    1964   'Pekah', *VT* 14: 121-35.

Coote, Robert B.
    1981   *Amos Among the Prophets: Composition and Theology* (Philadelphia: For-
            tress Press).
Cripps, Richard S.
    1955   *A Critical and Exegetical Commentary on the Book of Amos* (London: SPCK,
            2nd edn).
Croatto, J. Severino
    1987   *Biblical Hermeneutics: Toward a Theory of Reading as the Production of
            Meaning* (Maryknoll, NY: Orbis Books).
Cyril of Alexandria
    1864   *Commentarius in Amos Prophetam* in *Patrologia Graeca*, 71: 407-582.
    2007   *Commentary on the Twelve Prophets* (trans. Robert C. Hill; Fathers of the
            Church, 115; Washington, DC: Catholic University of America Press).
Davies, Philip R.
    2009   'Why do we know about Amos?', in Edelman and Ben Zvi 2009: 55-72.
Dearman, J. Andrew
    1988   *Property Rights in the Eighth-Century Prophets: The Conflict and its Back-
            ground* (Atlanta: Scholars Press).
Dempsey, Carol J.
    2000   *The Prophets: A Liberation-Critical Reading* (Minneapolis: Fortress Press).
Domeris, William Robert
    2007   *Touching the Heart of God: The Social Construction of Poverty among Bib-
            lical Peasants* (LHBOTS, 466: New York: T. & T. Clark).
Dorsey, David A.
    1992   'Literary Architecture and Aural Structuring Techniques in Amos', *Bib* 73:
            305-30.
    1999   *The Literary Structure of the Old Testament: A Commentary on Genesis to
            Malachi* (Grand Rapids: Baker).
Duff, Archibald
    1891   *Old Testament Theology, or the History of Hebrew Religion from the Year
            800 B.C.* (London and Edinburgh: A. & C. Black).
Duhm, Bernhard
    1875   *Die Theologie der Propheten als Grundlage für die innere Entwicklungsge-
            schichte der Israelitischen Religion* (Bonn: Marcus).
Edelman, Diana V.
    2009   'From Prophets to Prophetic Books: The Fixing of the Divine Word', in Edel-
            man and Ben Zvi 2009: 29-54.
Edelman, Diana V., and Ehud Ben Zvi (eds.)
    2009   *The Production of Prophecy: Constructing Prophecy and Prophets in Yehud*
            (London: Equinox).
Eichrodt, Walther
    1961   *The Theology of the Old Testament*, Vol. 1 (London: SCM Press).
Eisenstadt, S.N., and L. Roniger
    1984   *Patrons, Clients and Friends: Interpersonal Relations and the Structure of
            Trust in Society* (Cambridge: Cambridge University Press).
Faust, Avraham
    2012a   *Judah in the Neo-Babylonian Period: The Archaeology of Desolation* (SBL
            Archaeology and Biblical Studies, 18; Atlanta, GA: Society of Biblical
            Studies).

2012b   *The Archaeology of Israelite Society in Iron Age II* (Winona Lake, IN: Eisenbrauns).

Ferreiro, Alberto (ed.)
2003   *The Twelve Prophets* (Ancient Christian Commentary on Scripture OT, 14; Downers Grove, IL: InterVarsity).

Fey, Reinhard
1963   *Amos und Jesaja, Abhängigkeit und Eigenständigkeit des Jesaja* (WMANT, 12; Neukirchen–Vluyn: Neukirchener Verlag).

Finkelstein, Israel, and Lily Singer-Avitz
2009   'Re-evaluating Bethel', *ZDPV* 125: 33-48.

Fishelov, David
1989   'The Prophet as Satirist', *Prooftexts* 9.3: 195-211.

Fleischer, Gerhard
1989   *Von Menschenverkäufern, Baschankühen und Rechtsverkehrern: Die Sozialkritik des Amosbuches in historisch-kritischer, sozialgeschichtlicher und archäologischer Perspektive* (BBB, 74; Frankfurt: Athenäum).

Fleming, Daniel E.
2012   *The Legacy of Israel in Judah's Bible: History, Politics and the Reinscribing of Tradition* (Cambridge: Cambridge University Press).

Garrett, Duane A.
2008   *Amos: A Handbook on the Hebrew Text* (Baylor Handbook on the Hebrew Bible; Waco, TX: Baylor University Press).

Geller, Stephen A.
1983   'Were the Prophets Poets?', *Prooftexts* 3: 211-21. Reprinted in Gordon (ed.) 1995: 153-65.

Gelston, Anthony (ed.)
2010   *The Twelve Minor Prophets* (Biblia Hebraica Quinta, 13; Stuttgart: Deutsche Bibelgesellschaft). Page numbers with * are numbered from the right-hand-opening (left to right) end of the book.

Gese, H.
1981   'Komposition bei Amos', in J.A. Emerton (ed.), *Congress Volume Vienna 1980* (VTSup, 32; Leiden: E.J. Brill): 74-95.

Geus, Jan Kees de
1982   'Die Gesellschaftskritik der Propheten und die Archäologie', *ZDPV* 98: 50-57.

Goldingay, John
2006   *Old Testament Theology*. II. *Israel's Faith* (Downers Grove, IL: InterVarsity Press; Milton Keynes: Paternoster Press).

Gordon, Robert P. (ed.)
1995   *'The Place Is Too Small for Us': The Israelite Prophets in Recent Scholarship* (Sources for Biblical and Theological Study, 5; Winona Lake, IN: Eisenbrauns).

Gottwald, Norman K.
1993   'Social Class as an Analytic and Hermeneutical Category in Biblical Studies', *JBL* 112: 3-22.

Gowan, Donald E.
1998   *Theology of the Prophetic Books: The Death and Resurrection of Israel* (Louisville, KY: Westminster/John Knox Press).

Graeber, David
  2011   *Debt: The First 5,000 Years* (Brooklyn and London: Melville House).
Guillaume, Philippe
  2012   *Land, Credit and Crisis: Agrarian Finance in the Hebrew Bible* (Sheffield and Oakville, CT: Equinox).
Hadjiev, Tchavdar S.
  2009   *The Composition and Redaction of the Book of Amos* (BZAW, 393; Berlin: W. de Gruyter).
Hagedorn, Anselm, and Andrew Mein (eds.)
  2011   *Aspects of Amos: Exegesis and Imagination* (LHBOTS, 535; New York/London: T. & T. Clark).
Hamborg, Graham R.
  2012   *Still Selling the Righteous: A Redaction-Critical Investigation of the Reasons for Judgment in Amos 2.6-16* (LHBOTS, 555; London: T. & T. Clark).
Hammershaimb, Erling
  1970   *The Book of Amos: A Commentary* (trans. John Sturdy; Oxford: Blackwell).
Harper, William Rainey
  1905   *A Critical and Exegetical Commentary on Amos and Hosea* (ICC; Edinburgh: T. & T. Clark).
Hasel, Gerhard F.
  1972   *The Remnant: The History and Theology of the Remnant Idea from Genesis to Isaiah* (Berrien Springs, MI: Andrews University Press).
Hayes, John H.
  1988   *Amos, the Eighth-Century Prophet: His Times and His Preaching* (Nashville, TN: Abingdon Press).
Holladay, J.S.
  1995   'The Kingdoms of Israel and Judah: Political and Economic Centralization in the Iron IIA-B (Ca. 1000–750 BCE)', in T.E. Levy (ed.), *The Archaeology of Society in the Holy Land* (New York: Facts on File): 368-98.
Houston, Walter J.
  1993   'What Did the Prophets Think They Were Doing?', *BibInt* 1: 167-88. Reprinted in Gordon 1995: 133-53 (with the page numbers of the original in the text).
  1995   'What Did the Prophets Think They Were Doing?', in Gordon 1995: 133-53 (reprint of Houston 1993).
  2004   'Was there a Social Crisis in the Eighth Century?', in John Day (ed.), *In Search of Pre-exilic Israel: Proceedings of the Oxford Old Testament Seminar* (London and New York: T. & T. Clark International): 130-49.
  2008   *Contending for Justice: Ideologies and Theologies of Social Justice in the Old Testament*, rev. edn. (1st edn 2006, with almost identical pagination; London & New York: T. & T. Clark).
  2010a   'Exit the Oppressed Peasant? Rethinking the Background of Social Criticism in the Prophets', in John Day (ed.), *Prophecy and the Prophets in Ancient Israel: Proceedings of the Oxford Old Testament Seminar* (London and New York: T. & T. Clark): 101-116.
  2010b   *Justice—the Biblical Challenge* (Biblical Challenges in the Modern World; London: Equinox).
  2013   *The Pentateuch* (Core Texts; London: SCM Press).

Hunter, A. Vanlier
1982   *Seek the Lord! A Study of the Meaning and Function of the Exhortations in Amos, Hosea, Isaiah, Micah, and Zephaniah* (Baltimore, MD: St Mary's Seminary & University).

Jeremias, Jörg
1995   *Der Prophet Amos* (ATD, 24,2; Göttingen: Vandenhoeck & Ruprecht).
1996   *Hosea und Amos: Studien zu den Anfängen des Dodekapropheton* (FAT, 13; Tübingen: Mohr Siebeck).
1998   *The Book of Amos: A Commentary* (OTL; Louisville, KY: Westminster/John Knox Press). ET of Jeremias 1995.
2013   'Das Rätsel der Schriftprophetie', *ZAW* 125: 93-117.

Jeremias, Jörg, and Lothar Perlitt (eds.)
1981   *Die Botschaft und die Boten: Festschrift für Hans Walter Wolff zum 70. Geburtstag* (Neukirchen–Vluyn: Neukirchener Verlag).

Jerome
1969   *In Amos Prophetam, libri III*, in *S. Hieronymi Presbyteri Opera*, pars I, Opera Exegetica, 6: Commentarii in Prophetas Minores (Corpus Christianorum, Series Latina, 76; Turnhout: Brepols): 211-348.

Kaminsky, Joel S.
1995   *Corporate Responsibility in the Hebrew Bible* (JSOTSup, 196; Sheffield: Sheffield Academic Press).

Kelly, J.G.
1976   'The Interpretation of Amos 4:13 in the Early Christian Community', in Robert F. McNamara (ed.), *The Sheaf, Bicentennial Issue: Essays in Honor of Joseph P. Brennan* (Rochester, NY: Saint Bernard's Seminary): 60-77.

Kessler, Rainer
2008   *The Social History of Ancient Israel: An Introduction* (Minneapolis: Fortress Press).

Kippenberg, Hans G.
1977   'Die Typik antiker Entwicklung', in Kippenberg (ed.), *Seminar: Die Entstehung der antiken Klassengesellschaft* (Frankfurt: Suhrkamp): 9-61.

Knauf, Ernst Axel
2006   'Bethel: The Israelite Influence on Judean Language and Literature', in Oded Lipschits and Manfred Oeming (eds.), *Judah and the Judeans in the Persian Period* (Winona Lake, IN: Eisenbrauns): 291-349.

Koch, Klaus
1982   *The Prophets. Volume One: The Assyrian Period* (London: SCM Press).
1983   'Is there a Doctrine of Retribution in the Old Testament?', in James L. Crenshaw (ed.), *Theodicy in the Old Testament* (Issues in Religion and Theology, 4; Philadelphia: Fortress Press; London: SPCK): 57-87. Partial translation of 'Gibt es ein Vergeltungsdogma im Alten Testament?', *ZTK* 52 (1955): 1-42.

Kratz, Reinhard Gregor
2011   'Die Worte des Amos von Tekoa', in *Prophetenstudien: Kleine Schriften II* (FAT, 74; Tübingen: Mohr Siebeck): 310-43 (first published 2003).

Lafferty, Theresa V.
2012   *The Prophetic Critique of the Priority of the Cult: A Study of Amos 5:21-24 and Isaiah 1:10-17* (Eugene, OR: Pickwick).

Lang, Bernhard
1983   'The Social Organization of Peasant Poverty in Biblical Israel', in *Monotheism*

and the Prophetic Minority (Social World of Biblical Antiquity, 1; Sheffield: Almond Press): 114-27. Reprinted in Lang (ed.), *Anthropological Approaches to the Old Testament* (Issues in Religion and Theology, 8; London: SPCK, 1985): 83-99.

Lenski, Gerhard E.
  1966   *Power and Privilege: A Theory of Social Stratification* (New York: McGraw Hill).

Linville, James R.
  2000   'Amos Among the "Dead Prophets Society": Re-Reading the Lion's Roar', *JSOT* 90, 55-77.
  2008   *Amos and the Cosmic Imagination* (Aldershot, UK and Burlington, VT: Ashgate).

Long, Burke O.
  1976   'Reports of Visions among the Prophets', *JBL* 95: 353-65.

Lust, J.
  1981   'Remarks on the Redaction of Amos V 4-6, 14-15', in B. Albrektson *et al.* (eds.), *Remembering All the Way...* (OTS, 21; Leiden: E.J. Brill): 129-54.

Marlow, Hilary
  2009   *Biblical Prophets and Contemporary Environmental Ethics* (Oxford: Oxford University Press).

Martin-Achard, Robert
  1984   *Amos: L'homme, le message, l'influence* (Publications de la Faculté de Théologie de l'Université de Genève, 7; Geneva: Labor et Fides).

Mays, James Luther
  1969   *Amos: A Commentary* (OTL; London: SCM Press).

Mazar, Amihai
  1990   *Archaeology of the Land of the Bible: 10,000–586 B.C.E.* (Anchor Bible Reference Library; New York: Doubleday).

Meier, Samuel A.
  1992   *Speaking of Speaking: Marking Direct Discourse in the Hebrew Bible* (Leiden: E.J. Brill).

Mein, Andrew
  2011   'The Radical Amos in Savonarola's Florence', in Hagedorn and Mein 2011: 117-40.

Miller, J. Maxwell, and John H. Hayes
  2006   *A History of Ancient Israel and Judah* (Louisville and London: Westminster/ John Knox Press, 2nd edn).

Mills, Mary
  2010   'Divine Violence in the Book of Amos', in Franke and O'Brien 2010: 153-79.

Miranda, José Porfirio
  1977   *Marx and the Bible: A Critique of the Philosophy of Oppression* (London: SCM Press).

Möller, Karl
  2003   *A Prophet in Debate: The Rhetoric of Persuasion in the Book of Amos* (JSOTSup, 372; Sheffield: Sheffield Academic Press).

Na'aman, Nadav
  2014   'Dismissing the Myth of a Flood of Israelite Refugees in the Late Eighth Century BCE', *ZAW* 126: 1-14.

Neusner, Jacob
  2007   *Amos in Talmud and Midrash: A Source Book* (Studies in Judaism; Lanham, MD: University Press of America).
Nicholson, Ernest W.
  1986   *God and His People: Covenant and Theology in the Old Testament* (Oxford: Clarendon Press).
Noble, Paul R.
  1993   'Israel among the nations', *HBT* 15: 56-82.
  1995   'The Literary Structure of Amos; A Thematic Analysis', *JBL* 114: 209-26.
  1997   'Amos' Absolute "No"', *VT* 47: 329-40.
Nogalski, James
  1993   *Literary Precursors to the Book of the Twelve* (BZAW, 217; Berlin and New York: W. de Gruyter).
Novick, Tzvi
  2008   'Duping the Prophet: אנך (Amos 7.8b) and Amos's Visions', *JSOT* 33: 115-28.
O'Brien, Julia M., and Chris Franke (eds.)
  2009   *Aesthetics of Violence in the Prophets* (LHBOTS, 517; New York/London: T. & T. Clark).
Paul, Shalom M.
  1991   *Amos* (Hermeneia; Minneapolis: Fortress Press).
Polanyi, Karl
  1957   'The Economy as an Instituted Process', in Karl Polanyi, Conrad M. Arensberg and Harry W. Pearson (eds.), *Trade and Market in the Early Empires: Economies in History and Theory* (Glencoe, IL: The Free Press and The Falcon's Wing Press): 243-69.
Polley, Max E.
  1989   *Amos and the Davidic Empire* (New York: Oxford University Press).
Rad, Gerhard von
  1965   *Old Testament Theology. II. The Theology of Israel's Prophetic Traditions* (Edinburgh: Oliver and Boyd; reprint from 1975 London: SCM Press).
Radine, Jason
  2010   *The Book of Amos in Emergent Judah* (FAT, 2/45; Tübingen: Mohr Siebeck).
Rauschenbusch, Walter
  1912   *Christianity and the Social Crisis* (New York: Macmillan).
Reimer, Haroldo
  1992   *Richtet auf das Recht! Studien zur Botschaft des Amos* (SB, 149; Stuttgart: Verlag Katholisches Bibelwerk).
Roberts, J.J.M.
  1991   *Nahum, Habakkuk, and Zephaniah* (OTL; Louisville, KY: Westminster/John Knox Press).
Rottzoll, Dirk U.
  1996   *Studien zur Redaktion und Komposition des Amosbuches* (BZAW, 243; Berlin: W. de Gruyter).
Rudolph, Wilhelm
  1971   *Joel–Amos–Obadja–Jona* (KAT XIII 2; Gütersloh: Gerd Mohn).
Sanderson, Judith E.
  1992   'Amos', in Carol A. Newsom and Sharon H. Ringe (eds.), *The Women's Bible Commentary* (London: SPCK and Louisville, KY: Westminster/John Knox Press): 205-209.

Savonarola, Girolamo
    1971   *Prediche sopra Amos e Zaccaria* (3 vols., ed. Paolo Ghiglieri; Edizione Nazi-
            onale delle Opere di Girolamo Savonarola; Rome: Angelo Belardetti).
Schart, Aaron
    1998   *Die Entstehung des Zwölfprophetenbuchs: Neubearbeitungen von Amos im
            Rahmen schriftenübergreifender Redaktionsprozesse* (BZAW, 260; Berlin
            and New York: W. de Gruyter).
Schmidt, Werner H.
    1965   'Die deuteronomistische Redaktion des Amosbuches: zu den theologischen
            Unterschieden zwischen dem Prophetenwort und seinem Sammler', *ZAW* 36:
            168-93.
Schwantes, Milton
    1977   *Das Recht der Armen* (Beiträge zur biblischen Exegese und Theologie; Frank-
            furt: Peter Lang).
Simkins, Ronald A.
    1999   'Patronage and the Political Economy of Monarchic Israel', *Semeia* 87: 123-
            44.
Sloane, Andrew
    2008   *At Home in a Strange Land: Using the Old Testament in Christian Ethics*
            (Peabody, MA: Hendrickson).
Smalley, Beryl
    1931   'Stephen Langton and the Four Senses of Scripture', *Speculum* 6: 60-76.
Smalley, W.A.
    1979   'Recursion Patterns and the Sectioning of Amos', *BT* 30: 118-27.
Smith, William Robertson
    2002   *The Prophets of Israel and their Place in History*, with a new introduction
            by Robert Alun Jones (New Brunswick and London: Transaction Publishers).
            Original publication Edinburgh: A. & C. Black, 1882, rev. edn, 1902.
Soggin, J. Alberto
    1987   *The Prophet Amos: A Translation and Commentary* (trans. John Bowden;
            London: SCM Press).
Strijdom, Petrus D.F.
    2011   'Reappraising the Historical Context of Amos', *OTE* 24, 221-54.
Theodore of Mopsuestia
    2004   *Commentary on the Twelve Prophets* (trans. Robert C. Hill; Fathers of the
            Church, 108; Washington, DC: Catholic University of America Press).
Theodoret of Cyrus
    1864   *Commentarius in Amos Prophetam* in *Patrologia Graeca*, 81: 1663–1708.
Thiele, Edwin R.
    1983   *The Mysterious Numbers of the Hebrew Kings* (Grand Rapids: Eerdmans, 3rd
            edn).
Thiselton, A.C.
    1974   'The Supposed Power of Words in the Biblical Writings', *JTS* 25: 283-99.
Timmer, Daniel
    2014   'The Use and Abuse of Power in Amos: Identity and Ideology', *JSOT* 39/1:
            101-18.
Tomes, Roger
    2004   '"Learning a New Technique": The Reception of Biblical Criticism in the

Nonconformist Colleges', *Journal of the United Reformed Church History Society* 7: 288-314.

2015 *Interpreting the Text: Essays on the Old Testament, its Reception and its Study* (ed. Walter J. Houston and Adrian H.W. Curtis; Sheffield: Sheffield Phoenix Press).

Tov, Emanuel
2001 *Textual Criticism of the Hebrew Bible* (Minneapolis: Fortress Press and Assen: Royal Van Gorcum, 2nd edn).

Tromp, N.J.
1984 'Amos V 1-17. Towards a Stylistic and Rhetorical Analysis', in A.S. van der Woude (ed.), *Prophets, Worship and Theodicy...* (OTS, 23; Leiden: E.J. Brill): 56-84.

Vermes, Geza (ed. and trans.)
2004 *The Complete Dead Sea Scrolls in English* (London: Penguin Books, rev. edn).

Waard, J. de
1977 'The Chiastic Structure of Amos V,1-17', *VT* 27: 170-77.

Weber, Hans-Ruedi
1977 'Prophecy in the Ecumenical Movement: Ambiguities and Questions', in J. Panagopoulos (ed.), *Prophetic Vocation in the New Testament and Today* (Leiden: E.J. Brill).

Weinfeld, Moshe
1992 'Justice and Righteousness'—משפט וצדקה—The Expression and its Meaning', in Henning Graf Reventlow and Yair Hoffmann (eds.), *Justice and Righteousness: Biblical Themes and Their Influence* (JSOTSup, 137; Sheffield: Sheffield Academic Press): 228-46.

1995 *Social Justice in Ancient Israel and in the Ancient Near East* (Jerusalem: The Magnes Press/Minneapolis: Fortress Press).

Weisman, Ze'ev
1998 *Political Satire in the Bible* (SBL Semeia Studies, 32; Atlanta, GA: Scholars Press).

Wellhausen, J[ulius]
1963 *Die kleinen Propheten* (Berlin: W. de Gruyter, 3rd edn [1898]).

Wellhausen, Julius
1957 *Prolegomena to the History of Ancient Israel*, with a reprint of the article
(1878) 'Israel' from the *Encyclopaedia Britannica* (Gloucester, MA: Peter Smith).

Wendland, E.R.
1988 'The "Word of the Lord" and the Organization of Amos: A Dramatic Message of Conflict and Crisis in the Confrontation between the Prophet and the People of Yahweh', *OPTAT* 2.4: 1-51.

Westermann, Claus
1967 *Basic Forms of Prophetic Speech* (Philadelphia: Fortress Press; reprinted Cambridge: Lutterworth and Louisville: Westminster/John Knox Press, 1991).

Wolff, Hans Walter
1973 *Amos the Prophet: The Man and his Background* (Philadelphia: Fortress Press).
1977 *Joel and Amos* (Hermeneia; Philadelphia: Fortress Press).

Würthwein, Ernst
1950 'Amos-Studien', *ZAW* 62: 10-52.

Zenger, Erich
    1988   'Die eigentliche Botschaft des Amos. Von der Relevanz der Politischen The-
            ologie in einer exegetischen Kontroverse', in E. Schillebeeckx (ed.), *Mystik
            und Politik: Theologie im Ringen um Geschichte und Gesellschaft* (Mainz:
            Grünewald): 394-406.
Zevit, Ziony
    2001   *The Religions of Ancient Israel: A Synthesis of Parallactic Approaches* (Lon-
            don and New York: Continuum).

INDEXES

INDEX OF REFERENCES

OLD TESTAMENT

INDEX OF AUTHORS